FLOURISH

FLOURISH

GABRIELLE BICHEL

CONTENTS

I wish to acknowledge my mum, dad and sister who have always been there for me and have provided support, guidance, and love throughout this entire book writing process. I wish to thank my grandma Cathy who has always been an inspiration to me in the way she exemplifies the love of Christ to others and how she encourages me in my faith walk. I wish to thank all my friends who have helped me along the way. Specifically, Lydia, Chelsea, Nell, Nicole, Adam, Jenny, Joe, my housemates and Rowie. I wouldn't have been able to write this book without you all. I thank God that I have been blessed with beautiful people in my life who constantly point me back to Christ and His unfailing goodness.

| 1 |

You Are Like A Rose

'To my dear Sons and Daughters, you are like a rose with many petals. Each petal is something new and special. This rose will never wither (heavenly speaking), never fade, as it is vibrant joyful and loving. There are many roses in the field but each rose is uniquely different. Although some of your petals have been worn or torn, or you may even have some thorns, the Gardener will water and replenish your soul and renew your spirit. You are a rose that can't be hidden, can't be tamed, and you belong in My garden forever. I will give you all the nutrients that you need. I will fight off any pests or bugs that may want to hurt you. At times you may feel that you might wither away. You might feel like you are ordinary. But you are not! You are unique and very loved. You will blossom and bring joy to the hearts around you and help other flowers to bloom. Love your Heavenly Father.'

This is the first time I have felt the beauty of what it is like to have the Lord speak to me. To set the scene, I was at a 12-day Young Adults Discipleship Retreat (YADR), seeking the Lord after a trialing season. As I was journaling, these words just came to me out of nowhere. I slowly re-read the scribble and started to sob as the words leaped off the page and into my heart. What a stunning way to describe the relationship we have with our Heavenly Father. These simple yet profound words have been the mantra of my life. Alongside the Bible and prayer, they have shaped my identity and the basis of my faith journey. I am honoured that I now get to share this with you.

This idea of God being our Gardener, among many other roles in our life such as Friend, Father, Saviour and Healer has helped me to inevitably realise that in order to flourish in life, we need to let God be our Gardener and enable his word to nourish our soul. It is my hope and prayer that this book will help you to see your true identity as a rose in our Father's Garden (also known as the Kingdom), and that you may flourish with Him, no matter where you are or what you do. I will be sharing parts of my personal journey with the Lord in the hope that he may be glorified above all else. I pray that you may be inspired to dream with the Father for He is always with you, always for you, and is eagerly anticipating that life altering moment when you say *'yes'* to Him.

I want to spend some time expanding on this idea of God being our Gardener as it sets the tone for the rest of the book. There is a bible passage which aligns with God being our Gardener which comes from the book of John chapter 15 verses 1 – 4. It essentially says, God is our Gardener and Jesus is the one true vine and we must remain in Him It also touches on the idea that branches need to be pruned to grow more and they can't bear fruit without being constantly attached to the vine. While this passage doesn't refer to us as a rose, it does paint the image of God nurturing and pruning the branches (aka us) to make us more fruitful and to help us to grow. It also helps us to understand that we alone can't 'bear fruit' and grow into our full potential without remaining and relying on Jesus. By having a relationship with Jesus, we can grow and flourish as He paves the way for us to be in a relationship with our Father through His death on the cross.

To sum up the book in one sentence; I wish to expand on the idea of God as our Gardener who helps us to flourish into who He made us to be. Obviously, there is a bit more to it, so keep reading! God is our Provider, and we get to go on this crazy wonderful, adventure with Him. As roses are reliant on the gardener to grow, we need to depend on God for everything too. It is hard sometimes, but boy is it worth it. There are so many human words we can use to describe God in our lives but no matter how many analogies or pictures we have, He surpasses our understanding. He is so much more than our Gardener, Friend, Father, Savior, Judge. He is our everything! This journey that we are on is exciting because each of our stories are going to be different. Our growth journeys are a beautiful reflection of how God works in various ways and when we share our stories, it helps to paint a picture of His goodness. Even though our stories are different, we are united by the love of our Heavenly Father and how we get the opportunity to share His love with others. His love is far greater than anything we could ever imagine, and I encourage you to 'dig deep' into the things He has planned for you.

I am nothing 'special' per say. I am an ordinary short in stature 23-year-old who grew up in a small farming town in Queensland Australia. Yet God in his marvelous strength and glory is taking me on the adventure of a lifetime and he wishes to do the same for you too. He turns water into wine and the ordinary into extraordinary through His grace and through His son. I truly believe that my life would be incredibly boring and dull without the fearless and relentless love of Jesus. I am going to explain how I view my relationship with God; however, I challenge you to reflect on your personal journey with the Lord and how you see him at work in your life. We all have a story to share, a testimony of His love. I hope you may reflect and see His wonderous mighty hand in your life as well. So, buckle up, grab a coffee or a late-night snack and enjoy my testimony about how even during hardships, we can flourish with Jesus by our side.

| 2 |

God Is Closer Than You Think

One bright Sunday morning, my mum, grandma, aunt and I were sitting in our tiny church book shop. We were chatting about everything under the sun, while sipping freshly poured instant coffee and nibbling on cookies. Suddenly, without any warning, a book flew off of the dusty shelf and onto the cold floor with a loud thud. The thud was enormously loud. So much that I had to quickly glance outside to make sure it wasn't storming. I, admittingly am still afraid of thunderstorms so if it were storming it would have been quite an ordeal. I took a deep sigh of relief as the sun was beaming through the windows. I just had to be sure. After confirming that there was in fact no storm in sight, we all gathered around this strange book, perplexed as to what had just happened. The cover was facing down toward the floor, so my grandma carefully picked up the book and flipped it over. We all gasped as we read the title. I could not help but laugh at the irony as I read this simple sentence in big bold black letters. 'God is Closer Than You Think.' Naturally my first reaction was *woah... God is in this room right now'* as I was whipping my head around in all directions scanning the room. I am ashamed to say but, in that moment, I forgot all the important theology I was taught in Sunday school.

This simple, yet profound, sentence has been glued into my brain like no other. God is closer than YOU think. Let that sink in, God is closer than you think. God isn't just close to us when we are in church or when we are worshipping or reading our Bible or doing 'Godly things.' Yes, He is close to us in those times, but he is also close to us when we are grocery shopping or running or when we are eating that delicious piece of chocolate cake. This is the extravagant thing about God - He is with us and His Spirit dwells within us wherever we are. He meets us where we are at and He guides us to where we need to be, which is closer to His heart. I don't know about you, but I don't necessarily feel the presence of God all day, every day. Even though we don't feel it all the time, He is with us and His love for you and I endures forever.

I was going to name this book 'God is Closer Than You Think' but I felt too guilty knowing there is already a book out there with this marvellous name. So, I have decided to call this book 'flourish' for multiple reasons outlined later. For now, I hope you know one of the ways we can truly 'flourish' in our lives is when we *acknowledge* that God is closer than we think, and He is with us, always. In the mountains and the valleys, He is there. In the good times when we laugh until we cry and in the bad times when we cry until we laugh, He is there, right by our side. This is the exciting part about life, we get to live our ordinary lives alongside our Heavenly Father, our best Friend, our Gardener, our sustenance and life giving Provider, honestly the list can go on forever. God transforms our ordinary lives into something extraordinary through His blood and with His love. The crazy truth is, we do not have to do anything, He has already done it all through the cross. We just have to allow Him into our hearts and into our lives.

When I was about eight years old, I was (and still am), an adrenaline junkie. I used to love going on adventures, especially to theme parks. What's not to love about theme parks? The air is always filled with the aroma of fried food, with faint screams in the distance that cannot be masked by the music, and there are always lots of people, everywhere! One day, my family and I went to a theme park. As always, I was ecstatic about being there, and truth be told it was a fantastic day. The only downfall was the fact I was still too short to go on some of the rides. I mean why do they have height restrictions anyway? Apart from keeping us who do not reach the 5'foot mark safe, they just restrict the amount of fun we have, and in my unbiased opinion it isn't fair. Height restrictions aside, once the day was over, we had to exit the park through the huge pavilion. This pavilion was filled to the brim with last minute shops, food stalls and, of course, people.

My family and I were dodging and weaving through all the people to make our way out. Suddenly something caught my eye - the ice cream stall. I was frozen in my tracks. There were so many flavours to choose from. My mouth was watering as my mind was racing between vanilla and chocolate. I sheepishly turned around to tap my mum on the shoulder to beg for a final treat but the lady I tapped was not in fact my mum. Embarrassed and ashamed I frantically looked around to find my family, but they were nowhere to be seen. My heart raced as the thought of ice cream dwindled down to nothing but regret. All I wanted was my family. I felt completely lost, alone and directionless. I knew that without my family I could not survive, yet in one split second, the thought of ice cream was more important. In sheer panic I clung to a pole and started to shakingly sob. I was doomed. After what felt like eternity (but probably a few seconds), I looked up and there in the distance was my dad. I let go of the pole I had clung onto and ran into his arms. He scooped me up as I sobbed into his arms and he carried me to the car. I was safe at last.

There is a story in the Bible, found in Luke chapter 15, about a man who had two sons. One day, his youngest son wanted his share of the estate, so the dad, graciously divided his property and the son went on his merry way. He travelled to a distant land and spent all of his money on wild living. Then, a severe famine hit the land and he was left with nothing. I mean, this guy literally went from living in luxury to being jealous about what the pigs were eating. He was alone and afraid. In shame, he decided to go back to his dad's house. He thought his dad was going to be livid, but he was dead wrong. Verses 18 – 20 sum this up perfectly:

'I will set out and go to my father, and will say to him, "Father, I have sinned against heaven, and in your sight; I am no longer worthy to be called your son; treat me as one of your hired laborers."' So he set out and came to his father. But when he was still a long way off, his father saw him and felt compassion for him, and ran and embraced him and kissed him.'

Just as I was distracted by the ice-cream, the younger son was distracted by money and fleshly desires. I bet you can relate here too. Sometimes in life we get distracted by things that take us away from being with our Heavenly Father. We can fall into the trap of clinging onto earthly things, in the hope for something more, to feel safe, loved, accepted. In my case it was a literal pole, as I felt it was my only lifeboat in my panic state. The things we usually cling onto for security and comfort don't actually solve the problem as they draw us away from trusting in God who is our lifeboat. What are you clinging onto for security and fulfilment? Is it money, a relationship, status? If it is not God, are you willing to let go of these things and run into His arms? Notice in the story about the two sons, the dad, was filled with compassion and love for his son. He knew what his son had done, yet he embraced him with open arms when he returned home. This paints a beautiful picture of God's perfect grace. When we get distracted by our sinful desires, we fall into the trap of thinking we are not worthy of God's love. No matter what we do, we are worthy of His love because of what Jesus has done through the cross. We just need to be brave and willing to let go of the things we have been clinging onto and run into His arms. This of course is easier said than done. As humans we are kind of like sheep, we can get distracted easily and we need to follow something. Just like my dad left my mum and my sister Lizzy to come find me; our Father, the good Shepherd is willing to leave the ninety-nine to come and rescue you and me. We just need to be willing to run into His arms just as we are, sobbing and all.

| 3 |

The Lion And The Lamb

If you ask me what my favourite Bible story is, I will without a doubt, say it is Genesis Chapter 22. Now, if you are familiar with this story you may be thinking why in the world is it Genesis 22? If you are not familiar with this story well, let me tell you, it blows my mind every single time I read it and I cannot wait to explain why. My love for this story began one morning at precisely 2am. For some reason I could not sleep, and I decided to start reading Genesis to make me fall asleep. I kid you not, the whole purpose for me even reading this book was to make me fall asleep. God had a different idea. So, I started reading, or should I say skimming, over creation and Noah's Ark but then I got to the story of Abraham. Long story short, Abraham and Sarah were really old, and they wanted to have a child. They thought they were too old but God gave them a promise that they would bear a child. The mind-boggling reality was they had to wait 15 years for this promise to come into fruition. They had ups and downs throughout this time and even though they sinned God was faithful to His promise, and they eventually had a baby named Isaac.

Chapter 22 begins with God testing Abraham by asking him to sacrifice his only son. The one He promised him. Do you know what Abraham said? YES. He said yes. WHAT in the world Abraham!! As I was reading this it was like I had forgotten the entire premise of the

Bible. My heart was suddenly pounding as I was wrapping my tiny brain around the story that was unfolding before my eyes. Was Abraham going to murder his own son? Why would God say such a thing? It was a three-day journey to where the sacrifice would take place. The next part always makes me chuckle. I must have an odd sense of humour because in all seriousness this would have been incredibly hard for Abraham. But I can just imagine as they finally arrive, Isaac is like, *'dad the wood is here but where is the sacrifice?'* Abraham would have been like, *'Oh, child, little do you know'* as he was tying him up and placing him on the wood. What an awkward conversation to have. Abraham then pulls out a huge knife and is about to kill his only son when God intervenes and provides a ram as the sacrifice instead of his son. Then Abraham calls the place the Lord will provide. As soon as I read this I started to ugly cry. Imagine being so obedient to God that you would be willing to give up everything for him? What would you be willing to sacrifice for him? For Abraham it was everything.

The consequence of sin is death, which is why they had to sacrifice specific animals for the atonement of their sins. But in this story, it is like we are Isaac. We all have sinned and fallen short of the glory of God. We were bound by our sins and the things that are not of Christ. We were on the chopping block, sentenced to death. But because the love of God is so ferocious and strong, he provided the ultimate Lamb, which is Jesus, to die for our sins and salvation. If you have not connected the dots already, the ram or lamb in this story is Jesus. Just like the ram took the place of Isaac that day, Jesus took the place for you and me, the day when he was crucified. Jesus is the lamb that was slain for our sins so that we no longer have to worry about death. He is the ultimate living sacrifice for us all. One of the main reasons I love this story is because it implicitly encompasses the beauty of the gospel. I could honestly write the entire book about this one chapter as it has a multitude of layers, meanings and messages to explore.

You will notice that this chapter is titled the 'Lion and the Lamb' which is a common phrase to describe the character of Jesus. There are many ways we can describe Jesus in worldly terms, however, we need to understand He is more magnificent and glorious than we could ever put into words. It is often said that Jesus is the Lion of Judah, and one of the burning questions I always had was why does the Bible call the enemy a lion in 1st Peter as well? For context, First Peter 5:8 says the following:

'Be of sober spirit, be on the alert. Your adversary, the devil, prowls around like a roaring lion, seeking someone to devour.'

Revelation 5:5 says the following:

'Stop weeping; behold, the Lion that is from the tribe of Judah, the Root of David, has overcome so as to be able to open the scroll and it's seven seals.'

Wouldn't you have this question as well? One day I asked a beautiful lady named Patience why she thinks the Bible says such a thing. Her response left me speechless, she said "in 1st Peter it says the enemy is *like* a lion. Whereas, in Revelation it says Jesus is *the* lion of Judah." Note the words *like* and *the.* She continued to explain how the enemy is a counterfeit, and a fake, and is trying to be *like* Jesus but he is not. As a lion is '*the king of the jungle,*' Jesus is the one true King, and if we choose, we get to be citizens of his kingdom. He is the true Lion of Judah, ruling with authority and grace.

I previously went to Africa on a mission trip, which I will probably bring up again because it changed my life. I realised two things about two different animals on this trip. Firstly, I came to the realisation that my favourite animal is a donkey. I love donkeys. You are probably thinking this is an odd choice but rest assured there is a fantastic reason why. A local man came up to our group one day and pointed out that all donkeys have the mark of the cross outlined on their back. For the rest of the trip I persistently looked at every single donkey to see if it was true, and you know what, it is. If you do not believe me, I dare you to google it! The phenomenal thing about this is the donkey happens to be the animal that Jesus rode on his way to Jerusalem. Jesus didn't ride a fancy horse; he rode a donkey. I don't think it is a coincidence that they have the mark of the cross on their backs. This shows when Jesus touches something, it leaves something eternal. Therefore, when Jesus touches our hearts, it leaves a lasting impact. Unlike donkeys, the way people can see the impact of Jesus in our lives isn't by a huge mark on our back, it is by our actions and the way we love Jesus and love people well.

My second realisation about an animal in Africa, occurred on a safari. It was a typical African safari. I felt like I was on the Wild Thornberrys or on an episode of Wild Planet as we were all crammed in a little van. It was surreal seeing all of the elephants, monkeys, hippos and lions. It was also amusing to see other tourists, dressed in kaki with binoculars, nudging each other and pointing at the wonders in sight. What stuck out to me the most were the lions, because they were not what I was expecting. From all the movies I had ever seen, lions were always running and pouncing and hunting and doing cool things, like singing... These lions were not. They were sleeping, they were playing, they were rolling around in the grass having a grand old time. If you saw these lions, you would think they were big fluffy cats that wouldn't hurt a fly. The adrenaline junkie part of me was raging on the inside for some action, something for them to pounce at, a roar, anything! What did I get? Nothing. Absolutely nothing.

God taught me an unforgettable lesson that day. Often, when we think of lions, we think of ferocious, fearless animals. The king of the jungle striding in authority and power. I am not sure about you but when I think of lions the first word that comes to my head is far from playful or calm. Yet I experienced this side of them. Just like the lions, we tend to focus on one characteristic of God. We either see Him as some distant being that is all powerful and mighty and miss the intimacy and sometimes even playfulness of God. On the contrast we can hyper-visualise him as our brother and friend and we neglect the fear and reverence for Him as our King. Just as the lion can both be fearless and playful, our God can be our king and our friend, our judge and our father, our defender and our comforter. Take a look at your own relationship with God. Do you fall into one of the above categories? The way we can flourish in our relationship with him is to balance reverence and relationship. The beautiful thing about the gospel is that we can have a personal relationship with our Heavenly Father because of Jesus, the lamb that was slain. In saying this, we must never become complacent with who He is: the mighty Lion of Judah.

| 4 |

The Gardener Always Knows

Have you ever seen a flower take care of itself? Without the help of something beyond itself, such as sunlight, water, and soil, flowers cannot survive. A gardener is an expert at keeping plants and flowers alive. They know exactly when to water and prune the flowers to ensure optimal growth and beauty. Likewise, God our Gardener knows exactly how to take care of us, if we let Him, of course.

I was recently in Indonesia during their rainy season and let me tell you when it rains, it pours. One of my favourite things was to listen to the huge raindrops hitting the rooftops and seeing the lush green grass. Rain is a beautiful thing and coming from an Australian farming town I know how precious it really is. One day I was sitting next to an open window listening to the heavy rain as it poured down over the Indonesian city. I was in awe of the magnificent beauty of the thundering rain and I began to praise God. Suddenly, the rain stopped, and I was devastated. It was such a petty thing to be upset about, I know. But it was right when I was appreciating it the most. I prayed and asked God to bring the rain back because I wanted to listen to it again. A few moments later I felt the Holy Spirit say to me, *'I love you'* just as the heavens opened and it started to rain again. It was even more beautiful than before. As each droplet hit the pavement and the rooftops I felt undeniably loved by God. Such a small moment can have a massive impact in the Kingdom of Heaven, and this was one of those moments.

On another occasion, I was in a small village in Africa. This village was the polar opposite of Indonesia. It was like a desert. They hardly had any rain. In fact, they did not have any running water for at least three months prior. For our two-week stay we had no showers and we had to be very careful with the bottled water we did have. It was rough. I never thought I would ever have to pray for a toilet to flush but God often surprises us with the things we have to do. It was an adventure to say the very least, and although difficult I met some incredible people and have some of my fondest memories there. One day we decided to pray for rain. We got together and we prayed, we sang songs about rain and we danced for hours. Guess what happened. Nothing. No rain. We left the village defeated, without a single drop of rain. Three months later we found out the village finally had a substantial amount of rain. It was glorious.

If a gardener waters a flower constantly, it drowns. If they withhold water for too long, it withers. Like a good Gardener, God knows exactly how much water we need and when. Sometimes He may withhold something to prevent us from drowning, or he may answer our prayers straight away like how He did in the first rain story. He has perfect timing for everything, and He knows how to answer our prayers according to His will. For His glory. An example of this happened when I was younger. I always wanted a pet but my parents were dead against the idea. One day I prayed for a cat and the next day, I am not even kidding here, a cat showed up on our doorstep and we kept him for 10 years. However, this was not enough as I also wanted a dog. I pleaded with my parents for what felt like my entire life, and the answer was always no. I prayed to God for a solid 10 years on this one. Then finally, after 10 years, my parents sent me a picture of a dog and at first, I thought they were playing a sick joke. But it turns out they were telling the truth. They ended up buying a dog while I was away. My parents now have a wonderful, playful, sometimes crazy dog, named Penny and she has brightened up our lives for the better. Since

I have moved out, I now have a Golden Labrador of my own named Toby. When I named him, I had no idea that the name means, *'God is good.'* When I first found this out, I chuckled to myself and was in awe of God and His goodness every time I looked at the dog. It is a reminder that God answers our prayers according to His will, not ours. It is also a reminder that He is good, all the time. No matter our circumstance and if He answers our prayers or not. God knows what He is doing, we just have to trust Him wholeheartedly. Sometimes He answers our prayers differently to what we expect or necessarily want Him to at the time. However, I have always found that when He doesn't answer my prayer it is usually for the best. He can see the bigger picture. One morning I prayed for my conversations to be fruitful, and guess what? Somebody else started talking about literal fruit. There was an undeniable sense of confusion in the room as I started laughing because I knew God was answering my prayer His way. God has the funniest sense of humour, and He answers our prayers His way. We just need to be willing to trust Him through faith that He knows what is best.

| 5 |

Unintentional Tattoos

I woke up one morning and had a wonderful idea. I wanted to get a tattoo! I rounded up my friends and we spontaneously headed to the tattoo parlour. Throughout the car ride I was frantically scrolling through Pinterest for some inspiration as I had no idea what I wanted. Smart I know… Once we arrived, I had decided I was going to get some flowers tattooed on my ankle. My friend decided to get her tattoo first and the nerves finally started to kick in. As she was getting her tattoo, I suddenly changed my mind and I decided to get a tattoo of a cross placed on my inner right ankle. I was stoked with my decision. A few weeks past, and I woke up one morning and had the same brilliant idea. I decided to get another tattoo with my same friend. I decided I wanted to get the word *'adventure'* written on my arm and I was sold on it. Because, you know, I love adventure and all. As the guy started to prep my arm I started to feel uneasy, and then quite literally at the last millisecond I snapped. I changed my mind and decided to get a tattoo on my ribs with the symbol meaning, 'God is greater than my highs and lows.' Another great decision. A couple weeks later, I decided to get another tattoo for some absurd reason! As per usual, I decided what to get in the car ride to the tattoo parlour. This time, I wanted to get a compass on my ankle. I was fairly set on the idea. I provided photos of what I wanted but felt a little weird about it. Of course, as soon as I got there, I changed my mind, and decided to get the phrase, 'Spirit lead me' with an arrow on my outer left ankle. When I looked at this tattoo my jaw hit the floor as there were two things that completely caught me off guard. The first thing was the outrageous fact that the tattoo artist accidentally put the 'lead' and the 'me' together, so my tattoo actually says "Spirit leadme." This has been interpreted by friends and acquaintances as spirit lead line, spirit loading, spirit bedtime and I am not even joking…goat butter. At the time I was absolutely gutted but now it is something I laugh at too! The second astonishing thing about this tattoo was the realisation that I unknowingly got the Trinity tattooed on me forever. You see, each one of my tattoos were spontaneous in my worldly opinion, but they were planned by God. I did not plan to get any of them, yet they all happen to be on my body and glorify God who undoubtably orchestrated them. The ultra-mind-blowing factor is, the cross was tattooed on my right ankle and the God tattoo was tattooed on my ribs and the spirit one on my left ankle. If you were to draw an imaginary line between each of my tattoos, it would create a triangle with God at the top, Jesus on the right and the Spirit on the left. This is cool because Jesus himself says He sits at the right hand of God. This is a permanent message which demonstrates that when you trust God wholeheartedly and go with what He has to say, it will all come together to glorify Him even if it does not seem like it at the time. He always sees the bigger picture. He is our Gardener, and He always knows what He is doing. To truly flourish and grow as His children we need to trust the process.

Since the Trinity realisation, I now have two more tattoos. I first got a rose tattooed on my ankle in a time when I was severely broken by worldly circumstances, which I will get to later. I got it to remind me of my identity and worth and how we are God's precious creation. My most recent tattoo is a map of the world on my other ankle. After my last tattoo, I felt God speak to me about my tattoos again. This time about the specific order in which I had gotten them. First and foremost is Him and always Him. Our relationship with God should always come first, no matter the season. I think there is significance with the cross coming first because it is through Jesus's death and resurrection that we get to be united with our Heavenly Father. It is through Jesus that we get to have a relationship with God (second tattoo). Even when we mess up, His love is far greater than we could ever fathom. After Jesus ascended into Heaven, he gave us the gift of the Holy Spirt which is our comfort and our guide (third tattoo). Then, through our relationship with Jesus comes our identity as a rose or sons and daughters of the Lord most high. As we start to grow in our identity, we can follow our calling, which ultimately is to love God and our neighbours in unique and interesting ways, hence the map. Sometimes in life, we can get the order mixed up. Meaning, we may rely too heavily on our calling or status and use it to find our identity. Then, it's only after we feel like we have done enough, or we have 'fixed ourselves,' we may feel like we can have a relationship with God. Having this mindset diminishes the power of the gospel in our lives as it takes away the power of the cross and replaces it with our own strength and might, which inevitably fails. It is a somewhat selfish mindset as it is kind of saying we don't really need God to help or even, we must be perfect for God to love us. In all seriousness, He came to save us when we were lost, broken, sick, and alone. He came to heal the sick and to provide us with His grace and unyielding love. Honestly, it is undeserving, but He loves us so much more than our flaws and our imperfections which is why the power of the cross is so radical. Jesus died for you and me just as we are. We do not have to be in a certain job or suburb or studying a certain degree to have a relationship with God. We are accepted by his grace and it is through a relationship with Jesus that we get to form our beautiful identity. Jesus came to earth for the broken, the hungry, and the lost. It is the sick who need a doctor not the healthy, which is why we so desperately need Jesus as we are now. We are never going to reach perfection on earth no matter how hard we try, which is exactly the reason we need Jesus in our lives to help us to flourish and grow into the people He has created us to be.

| 6 |

You Think You Know

I am going to be blunt here and say there is a lot you and I just do not know. It feels good, to be right about something. However, just as much as we can be right, we can also be very wrong. As mentioned previously, a flower cannot thrive or survive alone. Yet, in our human nature, we tend to take things into our own hands even though we have a Gardener who will always take care of us. At the time we think we know what is best for us but God sees the bigger picture and He knows what is better for us. Sometimes what is better for us, isn't the easiest or the most convenient option. Rather it can be uncomfortable, difficult, and challenging. However, it is through these times that we can grow in resilience and character. God works all things for His good and His glory, even when we don't understand.

One Saturday night I felt a strange nudge through the Spirit that I was going to baptise someone. I immediately thought the next morning was my time to shine. I am not quite sure what my thought process was here, but I decided to make a two- hour trip to the Gold Coast. The next morning, I dragged myself out of bed as the sun was rising and I made the drive. I had no plan or specific destination at the Gold Coast, I just drove. I felt super spiritual that morning. I was blasting worship music and was praying. It was actually quite beautiful. I finally arrived at the beach. It was a great day, the sun was shining, it was not too hot and not too cold. Perfect conditions for me to baptise someone. I got out of the car, half skipped to the sand, and stood ankle deep in the water. I stood there as the waves were crashing over and over again. I stood and prayed and waited. The people who were walking past, with their pets and surfboards, must have thought I was nuts. I was trying to look around to see if there was anyone who would be nice enough to have a conversation with me. Suddenly my eyes pricked up as there was a middle-aged man off in the distance who was actually walking away from me. I have no idea what came over me in the moment, or why this was the man I chose, but I chased after this stranger as fast as my legs could take me. I felt like I was on Baywatch running fast but somehow in slow motion. When I actually reached the man I was puffing and panting like a steam train and my wild beachy hair was all over my face. Once I finally got my breath back and mustered up the confidence, I told the man that Jesus loves him so much. He looked at me, smiled, and said "okay" and walked off. That was it, that was the moment I had, and I wasn't sure if he could speak English. It still felt nice that I had the opportunity to tell him how he is loved by God. However, I could not help but feel a tad deflated as I was almost certain God told me to baptise someone. I was doubting my ability to hear God as I dusted the sand off of my feet and walked back to my car. I want to preface here that God may have used this experience in a different way to what I was expecting. It is better to have the courage to go out and share the love of Jesus than to not do anything at all. We can get discouraged because we do not see the fruit of our actions. I know I fall into that trap all the time. I think sometimes, we don't see the fruit of our actions so that we may trust and know that God sees, and He knows our heart. I also think gives us a heart check and it stops us from being prideful. God's plan is far greater than we could ever know or comprehend, and we need to trust that He knows what He is doing, even when we have absolutely no idea.

A few weeks passed and I forgot about my little adventure and I went up to North Queensland with some friends. We were staying near the beach, and it was stunning. While we were there, one of my friends were upset, so I went and had a chat with her by the ocean. We ended up talking about faith and life. One thing led to another and I ended up baptising her in the ocean. I suddenly remembered what happened weeks before and was sheepishly thinking to myself, '*oh... that's what you meant, God.*' Not going to lie, this was probably one of the coolest experiences in my life because my friend said when she opened her eyes for a split second instead of seeing me, she saw Jesus. To this day I one hundred percent believe it. If I am being honest, when she said she saw Jesus I was bitter and jealous. I thought, '*Oh man, why couldn't I have seen Jesus too, that's not fair!*' A moment later I had a mindset change and was reminded of the honour of representing Jesus to others. If you think about it, we get to show people Jesus everyday by extending love and compassion to others and by obeying His word. Even though people may not literally see Jesus when they look at us, they can see that our actions are different. They can experience the love and compassion we provide even when it does not make sense. They can see there is a fire inside of us, which cannot be hidden or tamed. We get the massive honour of being the hands and feet of Jesus in this world; but my question is, as Christians, are we living life as if people were to see Jesus instead of us? Are we being imitators of Christ?

God knew the entire time that I was meant to baptise her. The fact I got to introduce her to Jesus in a personal and powerful way was incredible. I got to witness her make a commitment to the Lord and it was such an incredible honour. I thought I knew what He was telling me and took control of the situation because I was too impatient to wait for the plan that would give God the most glory. We can often get trapped because of our love for instant gratification which can ultimately lead us away from the bigger plan God has for us or for others. We think we know, but often we don't. That's where trust, faith and relationship come into play. I don't regret telling the man that Jesus loves him, in fact I am glad I did it. However, in this instance, I can see how I acted out of my own impulses instead of waiting for God's direction and purpose.

I love telling stories, and in due fashion, I have another story along these lines I wish to share with you. One of my favourite authors is Bob Goff, and if you haven't heard of him, you should definitely read his books *Love Does* and *Everybody Always.* Trust me they are amazing. I think the reason why I love reading his books is because he always talks about all of his fun adventures with Jesus and how we can love others well. I was in the middle of reading one of his books and I suddenly had a thought, *'I wonder what this man actually looks like?'* On a side note, yes it was an odd thought but we are moving on. At this thought, I fumbled my way to look at the back of the book. When flipping through the pages, I somehow ended up seeing a page with all of his contact details. He is very bold for putting his personal contact details in the back of his book and it made me respect him even more. Immediately, I felt a nudge from the Holy Spirit, prompting me to contact him. At the exact same time my mum's phone rang, and she picked up the phone and said: "Hello Bob." At first, I brushed it off like it was nothing and kept reading my book. But over the following days I could not shake the thought. I felt like everywhere I looked I saw the name Bob. I felt like a little bit of a crazy person, however, in my defence, I did tell my friends and they were hearing the name Bob too. Finally, I thought, *'Fine God I will send an email to him.'* Brace yourself because this is exactly what I said, mistakes and all:

Hi Bob!!

My name is Gabby Bichel and I LOVE Jesus, people, coffee and adventure!

First of all (I know you'd probably get this a lot but it's true) your books are amazing. I'm in the middle of reading Everybody Always and it has blown my mind. Even though I don't know you personally, It is evident that the love of Jesus is at the core of everything that you do and it's really cool/inspiring to see! Keep up the great work.

Now, I've never really emailed a famous author so this is wild, but when the Holy Spirit tells you something how could you say no! So here it goes!!

Here is a little bit about me. I am 5 foot 1 so I look like I am 12 but I promise you I am 20 years old and I live in Australia. I speak the truth when I say I love the above mentioned 4 things. I love Jesus so much and without him my life would be very boring for sure. I love love love being around people. Like I don't know if you are familiar with the Myers Briggs personality test but I took it one time and it told me I was an ENFP and that I am 100 percent extroverted!!!! Crazy I know, I was shocked that someone could be that extroverted. I love coffee, but that goes without saying. And I love crazy adventures, especially when God orchestrates them because it turns into a testimony of how amazing He is!

I promised myself I would 'try' not to ramble because I can imagine you're a busy man with lots of things to do and you probably wouldn't have time to read the Gabby Bichel novel. (Unless you're on a 12 hour plane trip and you've seen all of the movies they have to offer, then you'd have no excuse but to read it... in that case I say you're welcome haha). So Bob, this time last year, I kid you not this is what happened in the space of one and a half months: I had my appendix removed, my gallbladder removed, I had an absis on my kidney, fluid in my stomach, cysts that they had to remove, I had all 4 of wisdom teeth removed, I had a mini car accident and my boyfriend at the time was cheating on me. What a time, right! Then long story short, after that God called me to do a discipleship training school through YWAM (Youth with a Mission) so I spent 3 months in the Pacific Northwest for lecture phase and for the 3 month outreach God called me to Uganda and Ethiopia, woohoo!!!! Uganda is an incredible country by the way, I loved it there. I think you made a good choice by investing in that country!

I am going to be real here and say I don't really know what God has in mind here, he just made it very loud and clear to contact you. Ideally, I would absolutely LOVE to meet you in person over coffee because... well you seem like a pretty cool man of God and speaking to you in person would be incredible in itself. But I totally live on the other side of the world so I don't know if that is going to happen any time soon haha! (And also the fact that you're a famous author and I'm a small town girl from down under). Anyhow, I finished YWAM about 3 weeks ago, In this season God changed my life completely. I really feel that God is calling me to go back to do a secondary school and staff and to essentially be a missionary. I know you don't know me at all, so I want you to know that I completely understand if you say no or even if you haven't gotten this far in the email! But If you are for some reason still reading this I would like to ask you to prayerfully consider if you would sponsor me financially to be able to go back and make a difference in this huge world. So I just ask that you pray and see what God says and if he says yes well... I would love love love to hear back from you. Even if he says no, it would be amazing to just hear back from you! I'm new to this whole thing so I'm just going to trust God and see what happens I guess!

Bob if you are STILL reading, first of all wow! Second of all I just want to say that I've grown up with the persona that I have to go to college and get a degree and a well paying job to be able to make something of myself, to be worthy. For example, My ex boyfriend once told me that he would never date me unless I finished my degree. I've finally realised that I don't need to do anything or be anything to be worthy, but I am already worthy because of the grace that is freely given to me. So I guess I am doing this radical thing because I fell in love with the people and the children in Uganda and God has planted a huge dream inside of me. My heart is bursting at the seams to be able to travel to more of the world and to share His love and joy with people. I've seen God provide finances for other people in miraculous ways, but unfortunately the society around me has not. Bob, I have had people tell me I can't do this thing, so I've been praying for God to provide the finances for me to do this in one of his crazy ways, so maybe this is a starting point... maybe it's not! But hey, God never stops being loving and faithful. He's pretty darn awesome as you already know.

Thank you so much for taking the time to read this!

Even if I never hear from you ever, I want you to know that you're awesome and your books really do change lives, with the help of the Holy Spirit of course.

I would love to hear back from you soon.

I wish you all the best for whatever the future may hold. God bless.

Gabby Bichel. (Oh and to pronounce my lastname it rhymes with pickle!)

Alright, so I assume you probably have a few questions after reading this. I even questioned myself after rereading what I had said. Firstly, yes, I did have a lot of surgeries in a short amount of time. Secondly, yes, I did take a test once and it said I was 100 percent extroverted. I will speak about both of these things later. Sorry about the spoilers. I want to share this with you because I specifically remember God telling me to email Bob, but I also remember what *my intentions* were. My main intention of emailing him was to get support to go on my mission trips. On the contrary, I don't think it was God's main intention for me. I misinterpreted what God had said by putting a selfish twist on it. Because God initially said to email Bob, my brain went on a rampage.

I started thinking that he would support me and I would never have to struggle financially again. But I was dead wrong. Looking back, I am extremely glad he didn't support me because God provided for me in a way that pushed me out of my comfort zone and drew me closer to him. Bob actually responded to my crazy email, and this is what he said:

"Great to hear from you, Gabby. It sounds like you're on a terrific adventure. Keep your eyes fixed on Jesus and write down everything you learn. You've got a book or two to write in you!"

What a mind -blowing response! At the time I was a tad deflated but also very excited because he responded. My internal response went something along the lines of, *'Oh my goodness he replied, yay how exciting! But WHAT? A book? All of the signs for this? He didn't even say yes or no!!'* My internal dialogue alone was enough evidence to prove the point of having a selfish mindset rather than a Kingdom mindset. Little did I know Mr Goff, who does not know me from a bar of soap, planted a seed in my heart that is now coming to fruition three years later. The beautiful thing is God takes our mess ups into account and He always gets the glory. I had no idea I would ever be writing a book, but God knew. Just as a good gardener knows exactly how to look after everything in His Garden, He knows what is to come and He knows exactly what we need. At the time I thought I needed Bob to sponsor me, God knew I needed him to tell me to write a book. Sometimes, we think we know what we need but, in reality, God sees the bigger picture and knows exactly what we need. The adventure is trusting him even when we don't understand.

These past two stories have outlined times where I have gotten it partially wrong. I now wish to outline times when I have gotten it completely wrong. I was contemplating if I should add these into the book as they are a tad cringy. However, I wish to show to you, we can get it completely and utterly wrong sometimes, but God's infinite love is so much stronger than our human mistakes. It is comforting to know that no matter how badly we mess up, or get things wrong, He still loves us. He loves us when we get it right and when we get it wrong. God is not going to abandon us when we mess it up sometimes in fact, He shows compassion and grace to us when oftentimes we don't even deserve it. One day I was reading the Bible, specifically Judges. In the book of Judges there is a story about a man called Giddeon, who had no special skills or qualifications, yet did some pretty amazing things with the help of God. I was reading this, and I suddenly thought of an organisation called the International Justice Mission (IJM). This organisation aims to prevent human trafficking all around the world. How amazing is that! Anyhow, because of how exciting it is, I assumed God wanted me to work there. Partly because I thought of it while reading the story about Giddeon but mostly because I was trying to mask my own plan as God's plan. I thought because I was reading a story about a man who did not qualify to be in his role, I should apply for a job that I did not have the qualifications for. Now I want to clarify, I do believe God can call people into jobs they have no qualifications for by a miracle. This was not one of those times. I immediately looked the job openings and saw they had a job opportunity. This wasn't just any job opportunity; it was to be the CEO. Yes, I wanted to apply for the CEO without having ANY experience in business. So, I spent the entirety of the next day perfecting my resume, writing a cover letter and preparing myself for a crazy adventure. I was convinced I was going to get the position as I thought God told me so. I sent my resume and eagerly waited for a response. During that time, I was dreaming about how famous I was going to be and how I was going to make an impact in the world. I was planning what car I was going to buy and the outfits I was going to wear. I mean I had it all sorted out. You will never guess what happened next... Absolutely nothing. I didn't even get a response to say they had received my application in the first place. I had gotten it completely wrong, and it is not the only time this has happened either.

A long time ago, I really liked this boy. One night I was lying face down in my room with the song 'I surrender' by Hillsong blasting through my brain as I was attempting to surrender this crush to the Lord. At this moment, I kid you not, I felt Jesus laughing at me. Not in a bully type way but in a way where a dad laughs at his kid when they mildly mess up because they don't know any better. I thought *this was odd* as I continued my attempt to surrender. The very next day I decided to go to a different church. It was around two hours away as I was also going to visit a friend. I again had to drag myself out of bed before the sun came up. I felt determined to go to church that morning. On the long scenic, Australian drive, I was praying. The prayer I prayed was, '*if this boy is at this random church today, I will know it is from you.*' When I pulled up to the church, my heart skipped a beat and then started pumping in overdrive. I squealed in my car. Guess who was at the church that day? The boy!! I quickly parked my car, trying not to crash from sheer nervousness and excitement. I looked in the mirror with duck lips and fixed my hair to perfection. I then gracefully hopped out of the car and approached the church. I casually said to the boy "Oh hey, fancy seeing you here." My insides were screaming. What makes this even more hilarious is that he sat next to me. My brain was going a million miles an hour and my heart was overcompensating to the point where I think I almost passed out. I remember thinking to myself, '*this is it, he is the one. Thank you, Jesus, you are so awesome. I wonder what my wedding will be like?*' This next part is really funny actually, this boy is happily married, to someone else! And they're a beautiful couple. He wasn't in a relationship at the time, but it happened soon after. Now I know why I felt God laughing at me. I mean, I laugh at me too, and sometimes cringe. I got it completely and utterly wrong and I will get it wrong again. I am sure you will too. These mess-ups prove God's plan, and His grace surpasses our understanding. Even when we get it wrong, He loves us just the same. Do not surrender your hope if you mess up. It is better to step out in faith when you think it is from God rather than to passively ignore what God is actually trying to tell you. As I mentioned previously, a gardener knows exactly when to water and take care of his garden. Flowers on their own can't thrive or survive without the gardener's direction and care. Flowers don't know what they need until it is given to them. God knows what we need better than we could ever know or understand for ourselves. I honestly just wanted to share my stories with you to remind you that we are human, and we do make mistakes from time to time. God isn't calling us to be perfect He is calling us to follow Him with open hearts exactly how we are. He isn't going to hate us for getting it wrong, rather, He pours out His love and patience to us.

Reading the Bible makes me feel better about my mess ups. Especially looking at the disciples. There is a story where Jesus and his disciples were in the Garden of Gethsemane. Jesus specifically told the disciples to stay up and keep watch while he prayed. What did they do instead? They fell asleep, not once but three times. Jesus kept on waking them up, but they continually fell asleep even after he told them not to and they knew it was important. Jesus didn't love them any less for falling asleep. In fact, He was about to perform the greatest act of love of all time by dying not only for them but for you and for me. So, in times when we do get it partially wrong, or completely and utterly wrong, we are forgiven, and we are loved. Jesus is taking us on a grand adventure and no matter if we get it right or wrong, He uses these experiences to help us grow and shape our Character. As I mentioned before, we do not have to be perfect, and we do not have to get it right all time, we just need to come as we are.

| **7** |

We Can Get It Right Sometimes

In the previous chapter, I spoke about how we can mess up sometimes. What a downer of a chapter. Sorry. This chapter I want to reassure you that sometimes we can get it right. We have the Holy Spirit dwelling within us, and because of Jesus we can have communion with our Heavenly Father. I do not want the last chapter to discourage you. I want you to be inspired to trust Him wholeheartedly even if you do make mistakes every now and then. Fear not, we can get it right!

I want to share another story with you. One where I actually got it right this time. One Sunday, out of pure curiosity, I decided to go to a different church (yes I was a bit of a church hopper). This church was quite charismatic compared to the traditional Lutheran church I have attended religiously since I was born. It was the first time I had attended church that month, so it was a miracle that I even decided to go to church in the first place. Nevertheless, it was a delightful service. During the service, the pastor stood up in front of the congregation of about 100 or so. In a stern confident manner he proclaimed, "Today we are going to say yes to the things God has planned for us." Not a second later the congregation starts chanting "Yes, Yes, Yes" In that moment, with the chorus of 100 'yesses' echoing in the background, the phrase *'summer camp'* strikes my mind like no other. My immediate reaction was 'NO,' yet there still seemed to be a melody of yesses ringing through

32

my ears. Again, in my mind I said *'no way'* as the yesses seemed to intensify and fill the room. After a few seconds of negotiating this new-found idea, I groaned, rolled my eyes, and said, *'okay fine'* and with that the room became silent and the service continued. I could not shake this whole summer camp thing out of my brain as it quite literally came out of nowhere. As soon as I came home from church I jumped online and lodged an application to be a camp counsellor in the United States of America. A few days later, I received an email stating that I was one of the top two candidates for the summer camp position. My heart leaped with excitement as I could not wait for this adventure to begin. Me, being… me, I told absolutely everyone about this. Friends, family, the shopkeepers, you name it! It felt like everybody in Australia knew that I was about to embark on a new adventure. A few weeks past and I did not hear anything about my application. A slight pang of concern twisted my heart strings as I decided to email the agency again to check on my application. A day later I received a daunting email that I did not want to hear. The other candidate was selected, and I was not able to attend summer camp with the organisation. A wave of mixed emotions came over me like a tsunami. On the surface I was relieved that I didn't have to leave home, relieved at the fact I could comfortably continue to live my life. I mean I had a scholarship, a stable job, a boyfriend, it didn't make any logical sense to leave anyway. In saying this, deep in the crevices of my soul I was disappointed because I thought I had heard a call from God. My response to God was, *'ha I told you my calling was to stay here. I knew I was making this up.'* I can just imagine God in this moment laughing and shaking his head saying, *"Girl you have no idea."* After this grim news, I had to awkwardly tell everybody that I was no longer going to camp. To top it all off I was heading to a retreat that weekend with a lot of people that I knew. At this retreat I had to explain to everyone the sober reality that I was not going to camp anymore. In the middle of this conversation, my dear friend Ben, who is also a Christian, looks me straight in the eye and says with authority, *"Gabby, you are going on that summer camp"* He then walked off into the distance. I was shocked at this response, I didn't know how to react, so I awkwardly laughed as I usually do when I have no words to say.

After a while, the news of the summer camp dwindled down, and it became a mere memory. My stable life continued as normal, until a few weeks later when Ben randomly called. I immediately picked up the phone and with no further question Ben blurted out "Guess who's going to summer camp?" Absolutely stunned and taken aback by the question I responded lightheartedly.

"Who?"

"You are!!" He exclaimed with excitement.

I completely froze, yet my heart was beating out of my chest. I could not believe what I had just heard. Was this really happening to me? Upon further conversation it was revealed that Ben had an American friend who went to his church. She happened to be the program director for a summer camp in the United States. She was living in Australia for a year. Ben talked to her and she talked to the camp director and he agreed to have a crazy little Australian join their summer staff team. Within three short weeks, I had dropped my jobs, my scholarship, my studies, packed a suitcase and boarded a plane into the unknown. During this time, God was undeniably patient, loving and faithful. He kept his promise, even when I had given up. He truly does work everything out for His good and glory, both when we get it right and when we get it wrong. All we must do is be willing to say yes to the amazing adventures he has planned for us.

Tears were streaming down my face as I hugged my parents and my younger sister Lizzy. Part of me did not want to let go. I was trying to savour the moment as I knew I would not be seeing them for a while. I took a deep breath as I gave them a final hug. My mum gave me a prolonged kiss on the cheek as I ventured off towards my gate. A mixture of excited and nervous chills were dashing through my body as this was the first time I was travelling by myself and over-seas (apart from New Zealand but it doesn't really count when you are from Australia). I boarded the plane and sat through an excruciating 14-hour flight. Once we landed, I was completely in the unknown, out of my depth. I was about to enter one of the biggest airports in the world, LAX. Naturally, as I departed the plane I sung 'Party in the USA,' an old school Miley Cyrus classic. I have never felt so much joy and excitement. I love new things and this trumped everything I had ever experienced. There were so many American accents, I felt like I was in the movies. I was completely lost but utterly amazed and filled with adrenaline. I tried an authentic burger from the glorious Burger King, and I was in awe of the busyness of this airport. My next layover destination was Minneapolis and I just happened to be on the other side of the airport. I gulped as I stared at my watch then at the board with the flight details. I still had two hours, but I had absolutely no idea of where I was or where I was supposed to be. I bowed my head in prayer and asked God if he could lead me to people who could help me. Sure enough, I met a lovely couple who were on the same flight as me and I was able to walk with them to my gate and board my next flight. Again, in Minneapolis I found myself completely lost. I prayed and asked God to help me. I suddenly met a security guard, driving a golf cart, who willingly drove me from one end of the airport to the other. Without him, I would have missed my flight, or should I say, without God, I would probably still be stuck in LAX. We are never alone when we have God and by trusting in him, we can freely flourish into who he has created us to be. I could not have flown by myself without him. In fact, I can't do anything great without him by my side. Trusting and abiding in Him is our greatest adventure.

After many hours of flying I finally arrived in Fargo, North Dakota. To be honest, this place was never on the top of my bucket list, considering I didn't even know that the Dakota's existed. But, I was stoked to be there because it was America! I was greeted by two lovely Americans who were waving a sign that said 'Welcome to NeSoDak.'

To my astonishment, I found out that NeSoDak stands for Northeast South Dakota, which happens to be the name of the camp. We piled into a giant car and they drove me to Target. What an experience! On the way, I saw yellow school buses and I yelped with excitement, "This is just like the movies." As we were driving, I noticed that the trucks were huge and we happened to be driving on the wrong side of the road. I felt like we were going to crash at every turn. We arrived at Target and I was exhausted but enthusiastic. Target had everything I could ever imagine, I was shocked that there was a grocery store inside Target and it felt like a dream as I glazed past everything. My experience skyrocketed when I ordered Starbucks for the very first time. I felt like I had an authentic experience as I sipped my caramel macchiato, trying to figure out which side of the car to enter. We drove to South Dakota and arrived at the campsite. It was so beautiful, but it was hard to take everything in because my eyes were burning from exhaustion. I unloaded my bags and headed straight to the glorious camp bed.

The next day, I woke up to a stream of sunshine glaring into my room. I popped out of bed with excitement and reassured myself that it was not a dream. I scrambled through my luggage to quickly change so I could head outside. I peered over towards the lake and saw a bunch of people singing and dancing around a campfire. I thought it was odd that they were doing such a thing in the morning, but I just went with it. As I was walking towards the commotion, I ran into the beautiful cook. She looked at me and said in her thick American accent, "Oh dear, you must be hungry, let me grab you some dinner." *Hold up... some... dinner!* I thought to myself as I properly looked at my phone for the first time. It was around 8pm. It was in that exact moment it dawned on me, the sun goes down quite late in the American summer. I was in fact severely jet lagged and had slept the entire day! She decided to give me a bagel with some eggs. It was my first time trying a bagel and I believe it was love at first bite. Seriously, bagels are delicious. I then got to meet the wonderful summer staff whom I would be spending the next three months with. I arrived in the middle of staff training so I was like the new kid on the block, but it didn't matter as everyone was warm and welcoming. The next three months of my life were a whirlwind, I experienced many things that were far beyond my wildest dreams. Every week there were new children nervously rolling their bags into the campsite to start their weeklong camp adventure and every week I had tears streaming down my face as I hugged those same children goodbye. One week I had the opportunity to go to Minneapolis and help lead a youth group mission trip. We got to serve an organisation called 'Feed My Starving Children' where we volunteered and packed food. We also got to go to the Minneapolis Zoo. It was a strange experience going through 'Aussie world,' and seeing all the kangaroos in enclosures, instead of my aunt's backyard. I got to experience my first ever baseball game, where I ate my body weight in deep fried cheese curds and cheered my heart out for the Minnesota Twins. I also got to go to the biggest mall in America, 'The Mall of America' (inventive name, I know). I have never experienced what it was like to be speechless until I entered through the doors of this mall. They had four stories of shops that seemed to never end. My ears suddenly pricked up as I heard faint screams in the background, and almost fainted with excitement when I found out they had a whole entire theme park in the middle of the mall. To top it off they had a Hard Rock Café, a Cinnabon, mall cops and an aquarium! This was a place like no other and I had never experienced anything quite as extravagant as this. Once again, I cried as I had to part ways with the teenagers I had met on the trip, but it was a reality I had to face often.

Summer camp consisted of lots of singing and dancing, often around a campfire where I had to avoid the smoke from burning through my eyeballs. It involved a multitude of bible stories, braiding hair, friendship bracelets, gaga ball, constant energy, and lots of coffee. It was my first time sleeping in a hammock, trying turkey, deep fried grizzly bear, deep fried oreos, learning guitar, and trying smores, which also changed my life for the better. I also found out that I love Dairy Queen cheese curds, which is probably why I don't have a gallbladder now. The little American children at camp were astonished with the fact that I was Australian. They would ask me lots of questions about my country, which I was happy to answer. Some of the children would ask with such excitement in their tiny high-pitched American accents "Gabby, Gabby, how do you say your name in Australian?" Or "Gabby, how do you say puppies in Australian?" I always responded with some made up word and they would always gasp and say, "Wow that is the coolest thing ever." I would then have to clarify with them that it was a joke while they ran away giggling.

Whilst camp was chaotic, and fun, and adventurous, we saw many children accept Jesus into their lives and realise what it is like to be loved by the Father. Beyond the fun and excitement, seeing children's lives transformed for the better was the best thing I could have asked for. I also met some of the kindest people who showed me unconditional love and took care of me as their own. There is one family in particular who let me stay at their house on the weekends, cooked for me, and even offered to do my washing. They showed the love of Jesus to me in ways I cannot even fathom and one of the greatest things they did was introduce me to my favourite holiday, the fourth of July. I am speechless when it comes to remembering this time of my life because God was with me through it all. His goodness and kindness to me was unfathomable. I will never forget how He worked in my life and the incredible people I have met along the way. I wanted to share this story with you because I want to encourage you to take a step of faith when you feel God speaking to you. Even if it sounds absolutely crazy, God has a plan, He can speak, and we can get it right if we trust in Him wholeheartedly. Even if we think we have got it wrong, He has got us covered by His grace. Saying yes to God that day in church was the best decision I have ever made, and it had opened the door to an abundance of adventures with God. I grew closer to God, I made new friends and I got to see His faithfulness in unimaginable ways. Was it scary? You bet! But I would not change it for the world. Before this trip I had no desire to travel or do anything out of the ordinary. I was happy being comfortable and I had no desire to change. God had other plans for my life, and it all started with a simple yes. Do you feel God calling you into something far beyond your wildest dreams? do you need to say yes to Him? If so, even though it is incredibly daunting, I encourage you to say yes to him because it will be the most amazing thing you will ever do. Sometimes, it will be difficult, and things may not turn out exactly how you plan, but He knows you better than you know yourself and He knows what you need. If I didn't say yes to Him, I wouldn't have this crazy story to write about, I wouldn't have been able to experience his faithfulness in times of uncomfortableness and uncertainty. He is Lord of all but is He the Lord of your life? If the answer is no, what are the things stopping you from saying yes to Him? Are you willing to say yes even when you don't understand?

| 8 |

The Chelsea

Chelsea is one of my best friends and she just graduated university with a double degree in business and science, majoring in accounting, mathematics, and statistics. She is so smart! I am the opposite. I am not saying that I am not smart, but I embarrassingly still need to use my fingers and toes to count sometimes. It's up to interpretation, and who you ask. Hence, I am calling this chapter 'The Chelsea' because I am going to talk about numbers. I told her I was going to name this chapter after her and she thought I was bonkers and could come up with a better name. I personally think it's a great name!

My favourite number in the whole world is 7. I love this number so much that I wish to write about it. On a superficial level, I was born on the 27th of August at 7:07am. There is also a great personality test called the Enneagram, which is essentially an assessment of nine different personality types. It turns out I am a type 7 on this personality test, and one of the online tests told me I scored 100 percent 7. There are 7 days to a week, and 7 continents in the world, which I love. I have been told that there are 7 sections of the Bible; law, prophets, writings or psalms, gospel and acts, epistles of Paul, general epistles and the book of Revelation. However, this is up to interpretation, obviously I am biased.

When reading the Bible, the number 7 always stands out on the page whenever I see it. Since I have realised I see it quite often, I decided to do some research on my good friends Wikipedia and Google. Did you know the number 7 appears in the Bible 725 times, (54 of those times are in Revelation alone)? Pretty wild huh? It turns out it is a significant number in the Bible symbolising completeness and perfection. Okay here is where it gets good (I will eventually stop throwing facts at you I promise). Now, there are 7 colours in a rainbow and there is a time in the Bible when God made a promise by using a rainbow. In Genesis, He promised Noah that He would never flood the earth again using the rainbow to signify the promise. What if, this was also to remind us of God's bigger promises and plan? Signifying that one day, He will come again to restore perfection and completeness in the world by sending His son. What if the rainbow is a reminder to us now that He will come again to restore all things? I am no Bible scholar but every time I see a rainbow now, I am reminded of Gods faithfulness to His promises and one day He will come again in perfect glory to restore all things. As you already know I love the book of Genesis, and this is another example of the deeper meaning pointing back to Jesus and His redemptive plan.

When I was new to reading my Bible, my friend once told me to not read Revelation. What did I do? Of course, I read Revelation first. When I first read it, my eyes were glued to the pages as it spoke about things far beyond my understanding. I have read it multiple times since. I am not going to pretend I understand all of what it is talking about because there are many things I cannot comprehend. I do wish to state the number 7 is mentioned quite frequently in this book. It speaks about 7 churches, thunders, angels, seals, trumpets, stars and so on. What is interesting is the number 7 is first mentioned in Genesis chapter 1 when God created the heavens and the earth over 7 days and said, 'it is good.' Then the number 7 is used frequently in Revelation which is the last book of the Bible. It seems to me like there is a theme of completion and perfection interwoven within the Bible. God intends to restore and complete His kingdom and we get to be a part of it! The book of Revelation also talks about the four corners of the earth, but what is interesting is if you take the four corners of the earth and you add the three parts of the Trinity to it you would get 7. Boom. It is practically symbolising the unity between the four corners of the earth and the Holy Trinity in perfect harmony. I write this because I want to encourage you to dig deeper into the Bible. It is the true and living word and it can change our lives and our hearts to be more aligned with Christ. There are many deeper meanings that go far beyond our understanding and we can never stop growing because there is always more to learn and discover.

There is a story in the Bible, in John chapter 11, about a man named Lazarus. He was Jesus' friend. Lazarus fell ill and died, and he was dead for four days. That is until Jesus came. Lazarus had sisters, Mary and Martha and they were filled with deep sorrow. But you know what? So was Jesus. It says Jesus wept. Then, the gravestone was rolled away and Jesus spoke with authority and said: "Lazarus come out!" Then, the dead man just waltzed on out of the grave, in his grave clothes and all. This story is powerful on a multitude of levels, and I will speak about it later on. For now, I wish to highlight something, which I found rather interesting. You see, Lazarus who was completely human like you and I, was dead for four days until Jesus rose him from the dead. Jesus who is completely God, rose from the dead after three days. If you have not put two and two together, three plus four is 7. This helps to emphasise the fact Jesus' death and resurrection brought completeness and unity with our Heavenly Father. It shows God's perfect redemption plan to bring His children (us) closer to Him and His heart. I don't know about you, but this blows my mind.

Another amazing aspect about the number 7 is, if you multiply three and four together, you get 12 which could also represent the 12 tribes of Israel, often mentioned in the Old Testament. I could possibly be reading into this, or it could be a huge revelation. Regardless, I do encourage you to study the Bible and to see the trends and themes that occur. Evidently, I am still discovering new things in the Bible. As mentioned, I don't think anyone can stop learning new things and growing from the Bible and their relationship with Jesus. It is what makes reading the Bible and living a life in a relationship with Jesus so exciting! This next story is a perfect example of how a well-known

Bible story can still bring new surprises and insight. There is a section in the Bible called the gospels and acts. The gospels consist of Matthew, Mark, Luke and John. I love all of the gospels but I especially love Mark. It is short and sweet, and it is jam packed full of action. If I were to be a gospel, I would be Mark. In Mark there is a well-known story where Jesus feeds 5000 people with just five loaves of bread and two fish. There are multiple reasons as to why this story is amazing. Firstly, what a miracle! Imagine being one of the people who had lunch with Jesus that day. It says they ate until they were satisfied. I wish I were there that day, I love bread and fish and well… food. I wish to highlight the word satisfied. They were satisfied with what Jesus had fed them that day. Just like in this story, our full satisfaction in life comes with having a relationship with Jesus and letting Him feed us spiritual food through His word and His Spirit. Drawing back to the overarching theme, flowers are constantly being nurtured and fed by their Gardener. With this type of care, you could say they are satisfied and can flourish. What aspects of life are feeding into your soul? Is it the word of God and what Jesus says, or is it what the world says? I encourage you to take a look and to see what is sustaining you and if you are fully satisfied. The reason why I mention this story now is because five plus two is 7. Woohoo!

If you are not into mathematics and statistics like Chelsea, I am sincerely sorry. I just love how the number 7 can bring so much revelation and insight about Jesus and His kingdom. There is another story in the gospel of Matthew which flows on from the story above. This time Jesus was feeding 4000 people. Guess how many loaves of bread He had this time? He had 7 to be exact! It also says they had a few fish, but it does not say how many. Jesus gave thanks, broke the bread, and gave it to His disciples to share with others. Okay stay with me here, Jesus, the perfect complete wonderful, beautiful Jesus, came down to earth and broke Himself on the cross for us so that we may be reconciled with the Father and be complete. And our role, is to share Jesus with others so they may be satisfied and sustained in Him, just as the disciples did with the literal bread. You see, it is dazzling because they started off with 7 loaves of bread. Jesus is, and always was, complete and perfect. He was broken just as the bread was broken so that we could all be saved and satisfied through Him. He did this out of His great love so we can take part in the completion of His perfect kingdom.

Keeping with the maths and stats theme of this chapter, I would like to shift the focus to the number 3 now. Imagine a triangle. With God at the top, Jesus on the right and the Holy Spirit on the left (flashback to my tattoos!). The image of the triangle represents what a perfect relationship should look like: full, complete, and loving. Each corner is its own, but they interconnect with each other to make a full triangle. Now imagine another triangle, this time label one corner with God, another with others and the last one with yourself. We have 3 main relationships in our lives. First and foremost, our relationship with God, then our relationship with others and then a relationship with ourselves. God paints the perfect picture of what it is like to have a perfect relationship, and we get to imitate it on earth as best we can. Sometimes we will fail in our relationships and other times we will thrive. We are blessed to have a loving Father that will help guide and nurture all of our relationships and to pick us up when we fall. There is a passage of the Bible that helps me scaffold how I should approach my relationships. You may know this passage, or you may have no idea what I am talking about. The Bible passage comes from 1 Corinthians chapter 13. It is commonly known as the 'love' chapter and here is a preview for you:

'Love is patient, love is kind, it is not jealous; love does not brag, it is not arrogant. It does not act disgracefully, it does not seek its own *benefit*; it is not provoked, does not keep an account of a wrong *suffered*, it does not rejoice in unrighteousness, but rejoices with the truth; it keeps every confidence, it believes all things, hopes all things, endures all things.'

You may recall, I previously mentioned the notion of God being love. I have heard multiple times from many inspirational people, to replace the word *'love'* in the passage with God. I can't take credit for this but Let's try it! God is patient. God is Kind. God is not jealous; God does not brag. God is not arrogant. God does not act disgracefully, He is not self-seeking, He is not easily angered. God keeps no record of wrongs. God does not delight in evil but rejoices with the truth. God always protects, always trusts, always hopes and always preserves. God never fails. Wow! What a breathtaking way to describe our God. One day I was reading this and thought, *'If God is love, and we are called to love others, maybe we could use this verse as a way to keep in check with our relationships.'* We have 3 main relationships to uphold and to love. So, we could ask ourselves these questions: Are you being patient today? With God, with others, with yourself? Are you being envious today? Did you brag about something, or are you walking in pride? Have you been dishonouring, self-seeking or easily angered? Who have you been holding a grudge against? I think you get my point here. I find when I answer these questions honestly, I come to the realisation that my answer is quite the opposite of what I would like it to be. Are you in the same boat too? If so, it's alright. To be perfectly honest, it is impossible for us to uphold this perfect love the same way God does. It's why we need Him so dearly. I am not sure about you, but I feel incredibly blessed that our Father is so forgiving and merciful to us. If we keep asking ourselves these questions, we can keep ourselves accountable and make sure our heart posture is pointed towards love. If we have love in our roots, we produce good fruits. Meaning, if we are operating out of love, our actions will exemplify what is in our heart. We can love freely because He first loved us. His love is like no other and He pours out His love all the time. Whether you go to church or not, He loves you all the time, anywhere. I feel His love when I go to church, yes. Although, I have found, it is when I am living my ordinary every-day life where He shows His love the most. One of the most vivid times I felt His love was when I was driving home, by myself. Nothing special happened that day. But, when I was driving, I felt like I was hit with a tsunami of His love. I started weeping by myself in my car because I felt incredibly loved by my Father. It was so intense I could hardly see. I should have pulled over, but I didn't. The people driving past must have been so confused. God loves us anytime, anywhere, and we do not have to do anything to earn His love. He just loves us for who we are. Open your eyes, He loves you! Because He loves us, we can share.

| 9 |

All About The Money

A few chapters ago, I spoke about how I was thankful Mr Goff didn't fund my mission trip because God had other plans. I wish to share these stories with you now. This was an uncomfortable time for me but it taught me about God's faithfulness and love. I wouldn't change it for the world. Now I look at these times with gladness because I can see how God was working all things out for His glory. Just as a gardener provides everything a flower needs to thrive and flourish, God provides us with what we need but it may not be what we initially want. I recently heard a sermon where the pastor said: "faith is not faith, without trials." This is inherently true! It is easy to say you have faith when you are comfortable but what about when you are extremely uncomfortable? What happens then? That's when the real test of faith comes into play.

I have had a job since I was 14, which means I have been somewhat self-sufficient since then. After summer camp in 2018, I felt called to do a Discipleship Training School (DTS) with YWAM (Youth with a Mission). So, I packed my bags and headed back to America for a six-month journey. This journey started with a three-month lecture phase. Which is where you learn about various topics such as the Father Heart of God, and Biblical Overview. It was based in the beautiful Lynden, Washington. I found out very quickly that Washington State is completely different from Washington DC as I embarrassingly had a brief moment where I thought I was going to the Whitehouse. After the three-month lecture phase, YWAMers then have the outreach phase which is a three-month journey overseas. Lynden is one of the most beautiful places I have ever seen, apart from South Dakota of course. I mean the mountains were breathtakingly stunning and every time I saw them, I could not help but praise God. I went in the fall which means there were orange and brown crisp leaves everywhere, pumpkin spiced lattes, and well… pumpkin everything really. I loved it. I never knew you could put pumpkin in so many different things. Now, of course I had all of the finances I needed for this school because it would be crazy if I had just shown up without it. Right? This particular school cost around $5000, which I had saved for and had exactly enough. When I arrived, I had come to the realisation that people just showed up without all of their finances. I thought it was absolutely insane and was secretly glad I was not in that position. I was not intending for what happened next.

One morning, I woke up bright and early and had decided to go to the gym for once. Still half asleep, I attempted to climb down the ladder from the top bunk I was sleeping in. Suddenly, I lost balance and had fallen off the top bunk and hit my head on the floor. My beautiful friend yelped 'Gabby!" and I told her to be quiet as I was afraid to wake everyone in the dorm up. (Not that the enormous thud wouldn't have already). Plus, I didn't want to make a fuss. As I dragged myself into the common room the lights were burning my eyes, my head was throbbing, and I felt nauseous. It was not a good sight. I was rushed to the hospital in my loopy state and was told I had a concussion. If you are American, you will understand this next part: American healthcare sucks. It is the most expensive thing ever and it really was just like the movies. I was bedridden for a couple days. I hated every second of it because I could hear everyone laughing and having a grand old time without me. I had a bad case of FOMO (Fear of Missing Out). I was told I tried to escape my room to play drums (which I cannot play) and be with everyone during this time, but I do not remember such a thing.

I do remember wanting to go on a stunning hike with everyone a few days later. I am not proud of this, but I pretended I was better than what I was so I could go on the hike. On the way to the hike I was sitting in the back of the gigantic American car. The atmosphere was buzzing as we were all excited to go on this stunning hike. Suddenly, our car came to a screeching, grinding holt. BANG. The car behind us rammed into our car and knocked us around. Oh, my poor brain. My head hit the window from the impact and I felt weird again. Now the accident itself wasn't that bad and no one was seriously hurt. But, once again, I was rushed to the hospital, three days after my initial concussion. To my shock horror, I was diagnosed with another concussion and I had to pay the price, literally.

After I recovered, my heart dropped as I realised because of these new expenses, I didn't have enough to pay for the school. I was hard-core freaking out because I was on the other side of the world with no money. I was quite uncomfortable to say the very least. I decided to make a Facebook post as a 'final plea' kind of deal because I was desperate. A few days past since the Facebook post and I heard nothing. Defeated, I was ready to pack my bags and go home. I was in the midst of eating breakfast when all of a sudden, one of the leaders came rushing over to say that someone paid $500 towards my trip, which happened to be the remainder of my fees. To this day, I have no idea who was so gracious. But, because of their generosity and faithfulness to the Lord, I was able to go to Africa. And my goodness, going to Africa was one of the most incredible experiences of my life. I will treasure the memories and the people in my heart forever. It completely changed my entire perspective on life.

Do you want to know the two biggest lessons I learned from my six -month experience? Firstly, during lecture phase, in America, I was brushing my teeth. All of the sudden, I felt God say to me in my spirit, '*you are loved.*' Obviously, I nearly choked on my toothpaste as I cried. I undoubtably believe God spoke to me that day. You're probably thinking, wow, what an expensive lesson, couldn't God say this to me in Australian when brushing my teeth? Well yes, but, I further realised we first need to know that we are loved by the Father, so then His love, which dwells in us, overflows whether we go to the nations or go grocery shopping down the street. Out of a place of being loved, we get to share the love with others. Yes, the whole experience was amazing, but this was one of my biggest takeaways. It was simple, yet profound. The second takeaway is, God always provides and is with us. Always.

Once I got back to Australia, I desperately wanted to go back to YWAM for a secondary school and to potentially be on staff for a school. Everyone thought I was bonkers, considering the amount of financial stress I had the first time. I met one of my good friends, Adoniqua, in Washington and I found out that she lives an hour away from me in Australia. We caught up regularly and spoke about going back to Washington with the little to no money we had. I was in a bit of a pickle because I had told YWAM that I was coming back but I failed to tell my parents. It was tough. I worked as hard as I could in the three months I was at home and I somehow managed to save enough money for the plane trip there and a little of the tuition. Now I was the crazy person. My parents, as most parents would be, were not thrilled with my decisions. They thought it was stupid that I was willing to go without the finances. And to be honest, I thought so too but my desire to go outweighed the fear. My parents are beautiful and wonderful, but they did not think it was wise for me to go. My dad told me that there was little to no chance it would work out and, realistically speaking, he was dead right. But I knew deep in the depths of my heart I was sup-posed to go. I thought to myself, the lower the chances of it working in our realistic world, the more glory God gets when it actually happens, which I have found to be extremely true. My friend Adoniqua was fret-ting about the finances as well. She, in faith, decided to go and then she miraculously received a cheque which covered the tuition. We were both set to go back for three months! It was a trialing season. I learned a lot about myself in this secondary school, both good and bad. It was a growing experience for sure.

Later, found myself in another pickle. I told YWAM that I would stay for another six months and staff the next Discipleship Training School, but again, I failed to tell my parents. I did not learn. I thought my first financial situation was uncomfortable, but this was another level. I was on the other side of the world, with no income, zero dollars in my bank account, and I owed YWAM tuition money for my school and now rent, food, and also a substantial amount of money for outreach. I literally had nothing. Not even travel insurance. Whoops. I was practically homeless in another hemisphere. As I joined staff, I was technically a missionary. Yet, I had no supporters because I was too afraid to ask people. Or should I say, I was too prideful to ask people because I didn't want to rely on others or God for my finances. I thought it was easier to send emails asking for support to famous people I have never met before like Bob and even Ellen DeGeneres. I felt they couldn't judge someone they did not know. Looking back, I also had a sense of pride when it came to my finances. I didn't want to look weak because I was poor and had no money and didn't want to ask for money out of fear of judgement and burdening others. I saw other staff write newsletters and send gifts to their supporters. I did absolutely nothing of the sort, which in hindsight I probably should have. Although I was acting out of worldly fear, God was still faithful, loving and good and He never left my side.

During this period of having absolutely no money, God provided for me in crazy unexplainable ways. As I have mentioned, I love coffee and Washington has exceptional coffee. One morning I was on a run to clear my head, and I felt the Holy Spirit say to me as clear as day, *'I am going to buy you a coffee today.'* My immediate response was, *'I don't believe you'*, as I kept on running. I got to my favourite coffee shop. I was about to turn around and run back home but I suddenly needed to duck to the loo. So, I entered the shop, and of course, I knew the first person I saw. He was an older gentleman reading his newspaper drinking his black coffee. Startled and surprised he looked at me and smiled. He said in his thick American accent, "Let me buy you a coffee." Then he went and paid for my coffee. Trying to hold back my tears, I thanked the man and accepted the coffee. As I walked back to the base, sipping my hot coffee, I started to cry because God was faithful to His word, even when my immediate response was unbelief. He provided the coffee for me that day through that kind man.

A week later, I still had absolutely no money. Not even a dollar. It was bad. The worst part being, it was my fault in the first place. The hard thing about being in Lynden was being surrounded by so many coffee shops. It was a blessing and a curse. I decided to go with my friends to a coffee shop, knowing I had no money. I was in line and I had my card in my hand. This specific card was a load and go travel card. Essentially, if there was no money on this card I could not pay for anything. I prayed over the card asking God if he could pay for my coffee and my meal. My heart pounded as I was ordering my coffee. The girl serving me probably thought I had something wrong with me. As I tapped my card, I held my breath and closed my eyes and suddenly she gave me my receipt and told me my order will be ready soon. I stood there in disbelief, holding my receipt eventually being barged out of the way by oncoming customers. What in the world? I didn't think it would actually work. I kid you not, for that entire week God paid for all of my coffees. Whether it was people offering to pay, or my card going through miraculously, or even the person serving me saying it was on the house, all of my coffees and lunches were provided for that week. What makes it even more interesting is my mother has access to the bank records for my travel card. She called me and told me about how there were odd transactions being approved on my account without having any money. In my selfishness, I thought maybe God paid for all of my expenses too. I went to the ATM and I tried to withdraw $5000 from my account. It was declined. I tried again. It was declined again. God knew exactly what He was doing, and He knew when to provide and when I was putting a selfish twist on it. He is amazing and I am thankful He did not put the $5000 on my card because I grew from the experiences to follow.

I still had no money and one day someone randomly gave me $20. It was the best thing to happen to me. The $20 felt like $2000 to me. I was so excited because it meant I could go and buy some food for the week instead of eating leftovers! I placed the $20 in my pocket and guarded it with my life. When I got into my room I reached into my pocket and the $20 was nowhere to be found. I turned the place upside down trying to look for it. Devastated, I started to pray and read my Bible. I verbally told myself God is my provider, not finances, which is 100 percent true. Evidently, when you have no money, on the other side of the world you have to repeat this sentence all day every day to remind yourself. Suddenly I looked up towards the celling and a tiny red ladybug caught my attention. I felt the Holy Spirit nudge to me to google the meaning of a ladybug and I did. It means fortune or provision. I laughed and, in that moment, I decided to trust God wholeheartedly with my finances even though I did not understand. The very next day, I received my $20 back. It turns out a lovely gentleman found the $20 and prayed about who it belonged to. Long story short, the money came back to me, and I was able to buy groceries after all. God works in amazing ways. Sometimes we do have those unique ladybug moments and other times He provides us with a job or speaks to us through others. He is amazing, no matter what!

Eventually, I had to step out of my comfort zone like I have never done so before and fundraise. At first, I vowed not to ask my parents because I wanted to prove to them I could do it without their help. Besides, they were dead against the idea of me being there in the first place. I was living in pride again. I eventually asked them, and they agreed to support me, not only that, God changed their hearts and they were fine with me being there. Amazing! My beautiful grandparents supported me and my church made a donation as well. I messaged everyone I could think of on Facebook. I had some people respond and some people not respond, which was absolutely fine. Now, I was slowly but surely getting by and I was seeing how God was providing for my needs. I was able to stay and staff the school and it was wonderful as I got to pour love into the students. I loved it! The YWAM base had a giving time one day and people who had no money themselves were donating money so that others may go on outreach. I was taken aback by the selflessness of these people. After the giving time, everyone received all of the finances for outreach! It was such a wonderful feeling. I skipped into the office to celebrate only to find out that the money donated had gone towards my overdue rent and tuition. My heart sank as I still owed money for outreach. I was heartbroken. Everyone was fully funded except me. I was quite embarrassed actually and I didn't want to tell anybody. I had a meeting with my team and I burst into tears. I was embarrassed, ashamed, and poor. I was meant to be their leader, yet I had nothing, and I felt like nothing. My beautiful team prayed for me and loved me. After the meeting, my friend, the one who saw me when I fell, offered to pay for the remainder of my outreach. I love her so much. I love God the most!! I was uncomfortable but God was with me and looking back I would not change a thing because I can hold my head up and say that God gets all of the glory. He always provides for His children and sometimes it's in ways we do not expect.

But wait, there's more. After everything was paid for, we were about to enter into the month of December. I was due to leave the country on the 8th of December, which means that I had to pay the rent for the month. I certainly did not have the money for it. A beautiful couple from my church in America, Margaret, Dan and their son Skylar, allowed me to stay with them for the eight days of December for free. They not only allowed me to stay with them, they set up an entire caravan for me, fed me, gave me constant coffee, and even allowed me to use their car. I was taken care of. This was not the first time this had happed. When I was in South Dakota, there was another beautiful family, Janelle, Toby and their children Thomas, Lauren and Sophie, who had taken me in on the weekends for free, fed me, gave me coffee and introduced me to my all-time favourite holiday, the fourth of July. Both of these families showed me, the foreigner, kindness and grace the same way Jesus did. I believe God provides in an abundance of ways. Sometimes it is in unexplainable miraculous ways. Other times I believe He provides us with people or families, who demonstrate His love to us when we need it the most. I am forever grateful for both of these families. But, I am even more grateful for my Heavenly Father who provides for me, and provides for you, in ways we cannot even fathom. He exceeds our expectations, time, and time again. He is our ultimate provider.

I ended up leading a team with my dear friend Izzy. We led a team of 11 wonderful students in Southeast Asia for three months. And again, I truly treasure these memories in my heart forever. I loved being able to pour into young people as they were pushed out of their comfort zones overseas. I love them all and it was amazing to share the love of Christ with those in another country. It was hard at times, being in charge. But, it was a riveting experience, and I am forever thankful I trusted God in the times when I wanted to give up and go home. I could not imagine my life without my Southeast Asia team and the memories we share. Thank you, Jesus, my provider. I want you to know He provides for you too! You don't have to be in another country without any money to see how He provides. We get to see it in everyday life! By the clothes we are wearing, and the breath we are breathing, we are constantly reminded of how He provides. We just need to open our eyes and see He is with us.

Oh yes, there is still more. The Discipleship Training School I was leading on had 3 different teams being sent out to different areas. My team and one of the other teams were in the same country for a while. The other team was in a little bit of a pickle. They had lost a small bag. Not just any small bag, but one that had $5,000 in it. Yep, they lost FIVE THOUSAND DOLLARS within the first few days of their three-month journey. What an ordeal. They managed to get through the trip, somehow. But nobody knew what happened to the small bag with the money. At the end of the outreach our two teams met up for a debrief before heading back to the States. We were staying in the same place the other team were in when they arrived in the country. Where they supposedly lost the money. After a few days being together, it was time for us to depart. Now, I had a few visa issues which I will explain in further detail later. In essence, the teams were set to go back to the States for a final week of debrief. However, because of this issue, I could not reenter the States without going to Australia first. This meant I had to fly back to Australia all by myself. I said my final goodbyes and ugly cried when hugging my team. And they left. But I was still there. Alone. I had a few hours to spare so I decided to hang out in the same place and process everything that had happened. Probably an hour after all the Americans left, there was a faint knock on my door. It was strange. I didn't know anyone, nor was I expecting anyone. I slowly opened the door and there was a lady half smiling at me. She was holding a small bag. She did not speak much English, nor could I speak the language. But in our brief exchange she passed me the bag nodded and said, "For you." Naturally I squeaked "Thank you," as she was walking away. Thinking it was a small gesture from our host, I opened the bag. I almost fainted when my eyes interlocked with a stack full of cash. Holy moly guacamole. *Could it be?* I sat in my room in shock, not knowing what to do. I counted the money and yep, there, in my hand, was $5000 of American cash. Now this is a pivotal moment here. As you very well know, I was severely broke. I had no money at all, and this was a lot of money to me. I had one of two choices; I could have kept the money all to myself as I was alone, or I could have let the YWAM base know. I churned through various ideas and after much deliberation I decided to keep it for myself and... Just kidding! I called the YWAM base and told them about the situation. I don't think they could believe it either. I took the money back to Australia and after a very long time (thanks COVID-19), I managed to get all the money back to the YWAM base so they could use it for their ministry.

I share this story because sometimes we can get tempted. This is an extreme scenario, but I am sure you have been tempted at some point in your life too. It's rough. We know the right thing to do but our human instincts crave the indulgent, selfish thing. It is funny because my first initial reaction to receiving the money was thinking that God provided it to me. In actual fact, He was testing me and my heart posture. If there is even an ounce of sin involved, it can't be from God. He is not like that. He is pure, good, and righteous in every way possible. We, on the other hand, can sometimes steer away from these virtues. The things we do in secret and the choices we make in private are fully known to God. If we do fall into the trap of temptation, He is not going to hate us forever. That's what grace is for. However, if we love Jesus, we should have the inner drive to be more and more like him every day. The love we have for God, and His love for us, is one of the greatest defence mechanisms we have in resisting temptation and sin. He is our Gardener and our Provider and His love for us outweighs all of life's trials and tribulations.

| 10 |

Hawaii

I have left a huge chunk out of my story in the previous chapter because I believe this story deserves its own chapter. As a recap, I went to Washington for six months, then I came home for three months, and then I went back for nine months in total. I wish to talk about the period of time that I was at home. This time was hard for me. My soul was itching to go back to my second favourite place on the planet, South Dakota being the first, of course. I managed to get my job back at the university in these three months, which is a crazy story in itself because they keep on taking me back over the years, time, and time again. I liked to say it was my holiday job to save for my other job: being a missionary. I was working at this job and trying to figure out a way to get back to America as soon as possible. Due to the fact I had previously been to America multiple times, I had a visa. To renew this certain type of visa I could send my passport in the mail and they could renew it for me. I was over the moon as I did not have to attend a traumatising interview with scary people searching into my soul. So, I gathered all of the necessary documents and compiled them into a nice envelope. I then gave it to my sister to send for me because, apparently, I was busy that day. I was ecstatic as I was mentally crossing off this hurdle in my list of things to do before I go. Time was ticking. By the time I sent my passport I had about three weeks until my plane was going to depart. In my world, I had oodles of time.

A week flew by and I heard nothing about my passport. I thought it was odd but shrugged it off and continued working. A few more days past and I still had not heard anything. Alarm bells were ringing as I came to terms with what was actually happening. I decided to go to the post office and sort it out. They were not very nice to me. But at least we found out what was wrong. Australia has two competitive postal services: Australia Post and Toll. I found out they do not get along, shocker. My beautifully packaged envelope was in a Toll bag, and my beautiful sister Lizzy placed it in an Australia Post letter box. When this happens, the two postal services do not touch each-others stuff, they do not send it to where it needs to be, it kind of just lingers. Guys, this is legit. This is Australia's biggest unknown rivalry. I decided to go to Toll. At the time, my cousin worked there. She tried as best as she could to locate it, but the tracking number was damaged. What makes this story even more hilarious is I forgot to put the return address on the envelope. It did not have my name on it, it had none of my details at all. At this point I had about a week until my plane was going to depart. I was freaking out and praying that God would make it all work somehow.

I had two options, wait and see if my passport miraculously comes in the mail or get an emergency passport. I wish I could say that I had enough faith to wait for my passport to show up, but I didn't. I decided to get an emergency passport. Adoniqua decided to drive to Brisbane with me to get my passport. Funnily enough, I got violently ill that particular day. I didn't let it stop me though. It was now or never as I only had four days to go and the emergency passport takes three days to process. It was a classic Gabby moment, leaving it to the last second. Poor Adoniqua drove me all the way to Brisbane and by the time we got there I was feeling much better. I managed to get my picture taken and pay a ridiculous amount for my new passport (which did not help with my financial situation). I was not going to rest until I was on that plane. I eventually got my passport a day before my departure. I then realised I had to apply for an ESTA on my new passport, which is a 90-day tourist visa for the states. When applying, my eyes bulged out of my head as I read the fine print. It said it may take 24 to 48 hours to be processed. Oh dear, if it wasn't my passport stopping me, it would be my ESTA.

The very next day, I headed off to the airport on another grand adventure. This time it was different because I had absolutely no idea if I was going to get to my destination or not. Literally, when we arrived at the airport, my heart leaped with excitement as I received an email stating that my ESTA had been approved. Nothing was stopping me now. I was going to the States… again.

The interesting part is yet to come. I have left out this very important detail. My plan was to head to the States a week early, fly to the Midwest first, and then road trip to Seattle with my boyfriend at the time. My flight plan was to travel from Brisbane to Hawaii, Hawaii to another island in Hawaii, the other island to Seattle, Seattle to the Midwest, and then drive from the Midwest back to Seattle in time for the school. Crazy plan I know, but I was ready for it. After what felt like an eternity, I finally ended up in Hawaii. Everything was going smoothly, I felt like I was a professional traveler at this stage. Then customs happened. I was lowkey freaking out inside because of my whole passport situation. I had no idea if I had the right visa for the school I was attending, and I had no idea what I was going to say to them. My nerves accelerated with every step I took towards the officers. Suddenly it was my turn. They asked me why I was there, and instead of telling the whole truth I blurted out, "To see my American boyfriend." Oh my days, this opened a can of worms. They interrogated me like no other and I had decided to not mention my secondary school with YWAM. Whoops. They then looked through my luggage and, to my surprise, I forgot the very important YWAM documents I had in my carry on. Flushed in the face, I had to sheepishly explain my entire situation to them. They did not appreciate it. They marched me into the interrogation room, I felt like I was on the movies. My brain was going into overdrive as I was trying to comprehend what was going on. As I was sitting in the interrogation room, I was staring at the clock. I had two hours until my next flight. The minutes felt like hours as I was praying that I would make my flight. Guess what happened next? I missed my flight. I had a lot of time to spend with God, sitting all alone in the interrogation room. To be perfectly honest, I was a little angry at God. I definitely thought I was going to get deported. Shamefully, my heart posture that day was not ideal. The glorious thing about God is that He is always loving and always moving even when our hearts are hardened. It was my own fault that I missed my flight, but as humans we tend to blame others or even God for our own selfish mistakes. Looking back, He always had my back, even when I didn't recognise it.

I spent about three hours in the interrogation room. The beautiful thing was the people who were interrogating me knew about YWAM. They were so loving and kind to me, they even let me into the country! As soon as I was let out of the room, I felt like I was free. But, I ran into another hurdle. I had to sort out how to get to the mainland. I spoke with Hawaii airlines and they kindly helped me book some flights to the mainland, for the following day. They could only get me to Seattle though. If I were to go to the Midwest it would have cost me another $600. I was not about to pay that much to fly to the Midwest and then go straight back to Seattle. I quickly booked a hotel in Hawaii and fled from the airport for the remainder of the day and night. My hotel just happened to be in downtown Hawaii, so I decided to explore the place. It was stunning, I loved it so much. As I was walking by myself, I apologised to God for the way I had acted, and I praised Him. I must be oddly wired but, it was really refreshing to go on an unexpected, crazy adventure. You could smell the sea in the air and everyone I met was warm and welcoming. When I arrived back at my hotel, I was happy. In the remaining hours of the night I decided to see if my insurance would cover the cost of the hotel. I reached into my carry on to-fetch the orange folder with all of my important travel documents. I nearly fainted when I could not find it anywhere. *You have got to be kidding!* I was completely stressed and preoccupied about my travel situation that

I left my travel documents at the AIRPORT! This orange folder had my tickets, my insurance papers, photocopies of my passport, everything. What an ordeal. I kneeled at the side of my bed and I prayed to God for some help because I knew I was not going to get anywhere without His help. I have proven time and time again that I cannot do anything properly without Him. Surprisingly, God gave me a supernatural peace as I drifted off to sleep that night.

The very next day I was excited but nervous as I was about to go into the unknown again. I called an uber and was sad to leave Hawaii because it is such a magnificent place. The uber driver came and he was so nice. I said to him "I feel so lucky to be stuck in Hawaii of all places." What he said next has stuck in my brain like no other. He said in his think American accent, "Gurl, you are not lucky, you are blessed. When you say you are lucky, you are relying on worldly things. When you say you are blessed you are giving thanks to God. Never say you are lucky. It is relying on chance alone, and nothing happens by chance. When something good happens, it is a blessing from above. Saying you are lucky takes away the blessing and leaves it to chance." He gave me this speech for the entire drive. I was awestruck in this moment. I was questioning who was the missionary, me or him? We are all missionaries if you think about it! I have no idea if he was Christian or if he was just spiritual. He was right though. When you say you are lucky, it is subconsciously denying God had any part of what had happened. To this day, because of that man, I try as best I can to say I am blessed, not lucky. When I got to the airport, I was a tad stressed because I had no idea what I was going to do. I sat down for a moment and then suddenly heard my name over the loudspeaker. They wanted me to come to the front desk. I thought I was in trouble again. But I was dead wrong. The kind gentleman looked at me, and then handed me a bright orange folder. Standing in shock, I could not believe what I was holding in my hands. I quickly opened it and was relieved to find all of my documents there. God is GOOD.

I finally boarded my flight to get to mainland America. It was a long time coming but I eventually made it. I was home again. I arrived a week early, so I just hung out and caught up with a few people. It was great. On the day before the school was due to start, so the day I was supposed to leave to come to America, I got an unusual phone call from my mother. She was like, "Gabby, Gabby, Gabby you will never guess what has happened." And I was like, "Mum just tell me already." I still cannot believe what she said next. "Your passport, it has shown up at our house, with the approved visa for America."

"What in the world! You're kidding me!" I exclaimed as I almost fell over. I put two and two together in that moment. Now I know what God was trying to achieve. He wanted me to go to the school, but absolutely not to the Midwest. The boy and I are not together anymore. I think we can both agree that our relationship was not healthy. God was preventing me from going to the Midwest because He could see what we could not. In that moment, I realised He took me on this whirlwind of an adventure to protect me and the boy from what could have happened. I am so thankful He did this. I am so, so, thankful for His goodness in times when I cannot see. He is good to us when we are blind in our sin or worldly ways. He is good all the time, He protects us and loves us as His own.

I convinced my mother to send my passport to me in America, and she did. I am not going to lie; I was fretting about my passport being in the mail again. But, by the goodness of God, my passport arrived to me in one piece. So, now I was in America with two passports. The passport I arrived in the country with was valid for 90 days, the other passport had an approved visa for a year. We decided to go into Canada then try and come back into the states with my other passport. It worked out well, Lynden happens to be only 10 minutes from the border. The entire time I was nervous but at peace. My mindset had changed from when I was stuck in Hawaii in the interrogation room. I knew that whatever happened God had everything under control. We drove into Canada and stopped at Tim Hortons (a Canadian coffee and donut shop), which was essential for the trip. We then turned the car around and headed straight back into the states. I was praying the entire time. Of course we got flagged and had to go into another interrogation room. As I was trying to explain my situation to them, they looked at me with wide eyes and confusion. I don't think they have ever heard of such a thing. It felt like years for them to decide what to do and I was preparing myself for the worst: to be deported back to Australia. They finally got back to me, and they said I could enter the states on my yearlong visa. However, if I left the States I would have to reapply for the visa. This meant I could stay longer than 90 days! I was overjoyed and relieved, but also scared out of my brains because as you know I did not fundraise one bit. I am incredibly grateful I was able to stay. Looking back, even though 80 per cent of the time I was nervous and uncomfortable, I am glad God took me on this adventure because He showed me His faithfulness and goodness in ways I cannot even fathom.

| 11 |

The Baseball Game

Would you believe me if I said this is the second book that I have written? You are probably thinking, it mustn't have been popular, or good, if I am only mentioning it now. It is kind of true and I will tell you why. God has placed writing a book on my heart for years. I would often have a plan and have no idea where to begin. Truth be told, if I wrote a book back when I wanted to, I would not have had enough content. Let's just say, God had to teach me a thing or two first. I finally started writing a book and I thought things were going well. I was about 40 pages in, thriving in the book. This is the most I had ever written, ever. Before this, my largest project consisted of eight pages, with diagrams. 40 pages was a hefty achievement. One day I was chatting with God, and I felt Him say to me that I needed to start over. I felt Him specifically say, *'your book is good, but it aint my book.'*

Those words spoke into my soul with conviction. I had two choices: to either continue with the book I already had or trust God and start again. I am sure you can imagine what my flesh wanted to do. I decided to trust God and start all over again. I could salvage a small sliver of my previous work, but most of it was canned. Sometimes in life, we think we are doing the right thing, but we veer off course and start to do our own thing. We get invested in worldly things and when God tells us to change direction, are we seriously willing to say yes? This is why trust is crucial in our walk with God. We need to trust Him with our whole heart because His understanding and perspective outshines us all. We need to trust His voice when He tells us to stay or to go. As you have gathered by now, especially using my own personal walk as an example, when we rely on our own knowledge and judgement, things do not turn out very well. We need to trust in our Gardner, our Father and our Friend.

When I think of the word trust, I always think of the Disney movie Aladdin (second to Jesus of course). There is one scene in particular that speaks to me on a multitude of levels. Spoiler alert. If you have not seen Aladdin the essence of the movie is a regular boy (aka street rat) meets a princess and with the help of a genie and a magic carpet he turns into a prince. I think you may be able to figure the rest out from here. The scene begins with the princess locked in her room. Aladdin rides his magic carpet up to her balcony. From her point of view, she cannot see the carpet and it looks like he is just flying. She walks out to him as he stretches out his hand and says, "Do you trust me?" She gives a startled look as he asks again, "Do you trust me?" She closes her eyes and takes his hand and jumps. She then lands safely on the magic carpet. You see, when we are watching the movie, we know the whole time Aladdin is on the carpet. If you watch closely, it shows she has no idea, she just has to take his hand and trust him. You can use this as a picture to help describe what it is like to have a relationship with our Heavenly Father. He is reaching out his hand to us, asking, *Do you trust me?'* and all we have to do is grab a hold of His hand and jump, knowing He will always catch us. Sometimes we may not see or understand, but He does. He always sees the bigger picture, we do not. This is why faith and trust are crucial in our walk with God.

When I first ventured off into the world, I started praying a specific prayer daily. It goes something along the lines of, "God, I pray for a crazy adventure with you. I pray for crazy stories that glorify your name. Amen." Obviously, I would add more to it, but this is the scaffolding of what I would pray. Little did I know or realise is, in most cases, in order to have crazy stories with God, we must be pushed out of our comfort zone and trust that He knows what He is doing. I love South Dakota so much that I decided to go back to camp. Yes, I have been a camp counsellor for two American summers! I am practically a citizen of the states… in my heart and without the green card. The second summer I decided to become a lifeguard. I am not going to lie the test was hard, the instructor was intense, and I looked like a dying seal trying to perform some of the mock rescues. I got to the states, with no dramas mind you, and camp NeDoDak was amazing. I fell in love with it, again. It was just as I had remembered it; the smores, the accents, the fourth, sharing Jesus and lots of coffee. This time I felt like I was a Baywatch celebrity because I was a lifeguard. A little camper from the year before remembered me. She came up to me and was excited to see me. She said she told everyone how Australians say puppies in a different way to Americans. The poor thing, she took my joke to heart and made it law for a whole year! I had to awkwardly tell her I was joking, and she looked absolutely gutted as she ran away from me. Let's just say, the second time round I did not joke about Australians having another language.

One weekend, a few friends and I decided to go to Minneapolis. It was a four -hour drive from the camp, but in our minds it was worth it. We decided to go and see a baseball game, I believe it was the Twins vs Redsocks. Obviously, I go for the Twins. We parked at the mall of America, one of my favourite places, and then we caught the train to the Target field, where the baseball game was being held. Of course I had my Twins jersey on, to blend in. I was also wearing a banana suit, to not blend in (If you really don't believe me, search up @adventurous_banana on Instagram!). I love baseball games as they are exuberant, American, and fun. Americans do this thing where the entire stadium chants songs about baseball. I was just mouthing strange words and making weird noises because I honestly had no idea what was happening. During the game, the most exciting thing happened. I got on the big screen, in my banana suit! My life was made in that moment. I was officially a celebrity. I was ready to sign autographs. My friends and I were over the moon, it was so much fun. On the train ride back to the mall, we could not stop going on about how much fun we had. We laughed and everyone was looking at us, but we did not care. Once we got back to the mall, we ventured to the car. I was still on cloud nine. Once we arrived at the car, my heart sank, and my happy bubble was burst. I had left my wallet on the TRAIN! This had my money, my cards, my phone, including all of my photos, everything. I quickly ran back to the train as fast as my little legs could take me. It felt like I had just chugged ten cups of coffee. As I arrived at the train it was taking off. I was running next to it with all of my might, and I caught the tiniest glimpse of my wallet as it escaped me. There I was, standing in an empty train station, in the biggest mall in America on the other side of the world with nothing. I was in so much shock I could not feel a thing. All of the energy drained out of me and I was following my friends around like a zombie.

My friends decided to remotely activate find my iPhone on my phone, but I was doubtful because I had no data, only wifi. Still mortified at the thought of what had happened, my friends allowed me to use their phones to contact people from home. I tried to call my parents with all my might, but they did not answer. I decided to call my best friend, Lydia, and she thankfully answered. I told her everything so quickly I had to repeat myself about five times. She could not believe what had happened, but at the same time she was not surprised. She then told me what time it was back home, and of course it was Sunday morning. This essentially meant my parents were uncontactable for the next hour or so because of church. My insides were panicking as I was trying to be cool. My friends thought it would be a good idea to distract me. We decided to go into shops and the entire time I was praying for some miracle. It was then that I felt God say to me, *'You will get your phone back, trust me.'*

Time was passing by quicker than the train that left. It was getting later and later. I was slowly losing all hope of ever getting my phone or wallet back. We all decided to get some food. One of my friends bought me A & W (an American fast-food place) and when he gave it to me, I cried. It dawned on me that I could not pay for such a thing myself. I bawled my eyes out in the middle of the crowded food court. I got down on my knees, with gunk oozing from my face, and I cried out to God for His help. The people passing by had no idea how to react to a young girl kneeling and sobbing to God in the food court, most people averted their eyes. I didn't care what people thought of me in this moment, I felt lost, alone, and broken, and I needed my Heavenly Father. Again, I felt God say, *'You will get your phone back, trust me.'* However, I was still having a major breakdown.

I composed myself enough to get up from the ground. It was getting late and we had to make a four- hour trip home. As much as we wanted to stay, we had to eventually leave at some point. Just as we spoke about leaving my friend got a phone call. There was a lady on the other end, her voice was raspy. She said in her deep pitchy American accent, "I've got cha phone, I'll meet ya at the mall in an hour." And then she hung up. I had a moment of relief, but I felt a twang of uneasiness. We of course decided to stay and wait for an hour and the suspense was overwhelming. Now I really did feel like I was starring in an American movie. We waited… and waited and waited. By this time, it was almost two hours since she had called, and we heard nothing. Out of curiosity, my friend decided to look on find my iPhone, and we almost fell over when my phone appeared. My phone automatically connected to the wifi at a Dairy Queen, which happened to be 10 minutes away. At this point we all scurried to the car and raced to Dairy Queen. My heart was pounding on this wild goose chase. Once we arrived, we forced the boys to go in and investigate. They marched into Dairy Queen and came back with nothing. They searched as best they could but there was no sign of anyone. Defeated, we piled back into the car and started to make the journey back to South Dakota. We assumed the lady figured out how to sell my phone on the black market and she backed out of the deal to return it. There was an eerie silence on the car ride. I thought I was going to get my phone back, I thought God told me so. We were about a half an hour into our drive, when suddenly my friend's phone rang. Our ears perked up at the sound. We answered it and this time, to our bewilderment, it was a different lady. In an enthusiastic bubbly voice, she said, "Hey! I have your phone." In this moment I was relieved and filled with peace. On the phone she explained to us how she was walking along, and these people were bartering off the contents of my wallet at a bus station. How it ended up there is beyond me. They were fighting over my phone and she walked along and pretended it was hers and thanked them for finding it. This lady happened to be nine months pregnant and at that exact moment her water broke. I am not making this up! She then went to the hospital and there she decided to call us and make sure it was returned to its rightful owner. She told us that she had lost her phone a week prior and someone returned it to her, so she wanted to do the same for me.

Once the phone call had ended, we all screamed in unison as we immediately whipped the car around and headed straight to the hospital. As the lady was in labor, she was not the one to return it to me. She sent one of the nurses out to the foyer with my phone. I ran into the hospital and almost tackled the nurse as I hugged her tightly. She handed me my phone and I thanked her dearly. I waltzed back into the car and we were all over the moon and quite frankly stunned with what had just happened. God, my beautiful Father, was faithful to His word and I got my phone back. Just like the Aladdin story, God could see everything, He knew what was going on, I just had to hold his hand and trust He would help me.

My beautiful friend Lydia managed to contact my parents for me, and she told them the story. My mother immediately deactivated all of my cards and no money was stolen from me. She then sent a new card in the mail. As I reflect on this day a few things come to my attention. First of all, I distinctly remember I used to carry my passport around in my wallet with me everywhere. But, that particular morning, for some strange reason, I took it out of my wallet and left it back at the camp. I believe God influenced that too! Secondly, I came to the realisation that I implicitly prayed for such a thing to happen. God was like, *'you want a crazy adventure? Here you go Gabby.'* Thirdly, I realised if the first lady didn't call me, I probably would not have gotten my phone back because we would have been in South Dakota by the time the second lady called. God works all things out for His glory. People often ask me: *how do you survive overseas?* And I often say, it is because God always takes care of me, even when I make mistakes and have no idea what is going on. He is an all knowing all loving Gardener, who takes care of me. Because of His great love, I have grown into the person I am today and can flourish into who He created me to be. He wishes to do the same for you too, you just need to be willing to take His hand and trust in Him.

| 12 |

Check Your Attitude

Being in Africa and Southeast Asia really makes you question your attitude and gratitude. Before I went to these places, I was a tad materialistic, but I had no idea. When I travelled to these countries, I had to sleep on floors, sometimes next to mooing cows, or cuddled up next to my friends for warmth. I went weeks without having a shower in Africa and had to use terrifying squatty potties in Southeast Asia. I was stretched to the limits, but I absolutely loved it at the same time. One of the ways I was stretched was with birds. I am terrified of birds. In Uganda they have this type of bird, it has enormous sticks for legs and when they stand they are taller than me (mind you it's not that hard). Their wings could wrap me up, and I reckon they could have carried me away. They were the most atrocious thing I have ever seen, I am not joking. When one flapped next to me I shed a tear of terror. Speaking of birds, I was mortified in Africa when I witnessed a chicken get its head chopped off. Then, I went to Southeast Asia. I had this moment where my legs turned to jelly and nearly collapsed with fear when the fearless ladies handed me a knife and told me to do the same. It wasn't just one one but TWENTY chickens. I had to chop the head off of twenty chickens. God loves to nudge you out of your comfort zone if you let him!

I walked through the slums in Africa, which absolutely broke my heart into a million pieces. I taught English to children who came from families who were involved in prostitution, which again broke my heart into a million pieces. Seeing people suffering hurts. It's overwhelming. I felt guilty for having a family who loves me and a place to live. I felt guilty for having a bed, clothes, a car. I do not think we are supposed to feel guilty for having things and I firmly believe God blesses us with things. I do think there is a problem when we idolise the things we have over God and when our heart is postured toward entitlement instead of thankfulness. There is a story in Exodus about how the Israelites were slaves in Egypt and God, being the mighty God He is, set them free! God did the impossible so they could live freely with Him. But, when they were in the desert their attitudes were not centred towards Him. In fact, it was quite the opposite. They had false gods and idols, they rebelled, and they even whined saying, *'Take us back to Egypt.'* Although God was angry with their actions, He loved them through it all. The problem the Israelites had was they put worldly things above God and then blamed God for the suffering they were enduring. The mind-boggling thing is God was with them the entire time. You see, when I read this story, oftentimes, I think to myself, *'How could the Israelites be so silly, God was obviously with them and they still rebelled and had poor attitudes? I would have never done such a thing.'* Then the Almighty God, in a tender loving manner, tells me to examine my own heart. Oh boy. There have been times when I have put people, things, and circumstances above God and other times when I have blamed God for the suffering I have endured. Our goal is to have the same attitude as Jesus, but sometimes it is hard. The astonishing thing is when we fall short, Jesus is there to pick us up because He loves us even when our attitudes do not reflect who He is. It is one of the many beautiful aspects of the gospel and the wonderful thing about Jesus.

When I think of the word 'attitude' there are many stories and people who come flooding into my mind. One of the people who inspire me the most in this area is one of my friends, Adoniqua. I love her dearly. When we first met in YWAM, we weren't exactly friends, and we weren't exactly enemies, we just tolerated each other. Adoniqua was fasting one day in the girls dorm room and she was sitting on her bed praying by herself. I barged into the room to get something and noticed her. Instead of letting her be, I sat on her bed and we started actually talking to each other. Let's just say since then, we have become great friends. I truly believe God set this friendship up and I am forever thankful. Adoniqua was on team Africa and it was about two or three weeks until we were set to leave. There was an atmosphere of nerves and excitement as it started to dawn on us that we were about to embark on a grand adventure together. In Washington it rains quite a lot and there happened to be lots of stairs where we were staying. One morning, bright and early, Adoniqua was on her way to worship practice when she tripped and fell on the slippery stairs. She severely hurt her ankle. When I arrived at worship, I was wondering why she was leading whilst sitting on a chair, it didn't take too long until I put two and two together. I still cannot believe she led worship that day. She was eventually given crutches and was hopping around like a kangaroo… sort of. She went to various appointments and the doctors were concerned she might need surgery. It was the week we were due to leave, and she received the grim news she might not be able to go to Africa. Personally, when I heard the news I was gutted, I can't even fathom what she must have felt. But, when I spoke with her over

Vegemite bagels, she seemed peaceful and calm about it and told me God is in control. In that moment I felt like a cartoon character as my jaw almost hit the ground and my eyes bulged out of my head. I could not believe what she had just said. The very next day she found out she could go to Africa and we all were relieved and filled with joy. Flying to Africa was the next challenge. She was given a wheelchair at every airport, which was fun for us because we got to wheel her around. She had a smile on her face the entire time. The actual flying part was the polar opposite and an absolute nightmare. I sat next to her on every single flight and I sincerely felt sorry for her the entire time. Not only was her foot throbbing from the altitude and the flying, but she was terribly sick. She couldn't just go to the bathroom whenever she liked. No, no, no…. She had to painfully sit and endure it and I had to sit there and endure it with her. We certainly became closer friends that day. Once we landed, she was still happy to be there.

We finally arrived in Africa and it was an extreme whirlwind. Once we got through customs, we went to the baggage claim. We started grabbing everyone's bags. One by one the trolleys started to pile up with bags and it almost looked like we were ready to go. As the bags were moving along and dwindling down to nothing, we realised we were missing a few bags and Adoniqua's was one of them. I could not believe it, and I don't think anyone else could either. What a turn of events. Our team had to make multiple trips back to the airport in the first week of being in Africa. We started to get most of our bags back and after about two weeks we got all the bags back but one. Guess who did not get their bag back. Adoniqua. She went the entire 10 weeks in Africa without her bag. She had nothing, and for at least a quarter of the trip she was on crutches. She pretty much lost everything she had on this trip, but she gained memories, which would last a lifetime. She also gained a wonderful Godly husband who goes by the name of Handsome K. She was a little sad, as you would be. But, her attitude and trust in God inspired me like no other. I mean this girl was living on the bare minimum, in pain, and away from home. I barely heard her complain and she willingly gave her heart to the people and to the ministry. We talk about Africa all of the time and she speaks about how amazing it was. She almost never brings up her struggles unless she makes a joke about it. I have never met anyone like her and just thinking about how peaceful and happy she was on the trip reminds me of where our true joy comes from. It's not from our things rather it is from the Lord our Sustainer and our Provider. The joy of the Lord is our ultimate strength.

When in Africa, we had the opportunity to stay with children. They were all extremely beautiful, inside and out, and they also taught me a thing or two about attitude. The children had nothing, their clothes were too big or too small or ripped, most had no shoes, but they had massive smiles and massive hearts. Some nights we would all gather outside and sing worship songs together. One night in particular, all of the children and adults were singing praises. We then sang one song that has stuck with me forever. It is called, 'I am blessed.' And the lyrics go something along the lines of *'I am blessed, I am blessed I am blessed x3'* and then, *'I don't deserve it but yet I am blessed.'* We were singing this song and as I looked around, I saw around 20 little African children singing this song with all of their hearts. The chorus of 'I am blessed' filled the atmosphere. I started to cry and cover it up because I didn't want to ruin the moment. Some of these children have had an excruciatingly tough life, yet they were singing about how they were blessed. It just brought Matthew chapter 5: 3-10 to life for me where it says:

'Blessed are the poor in spirit, for theirs is the kingdom of heaven. Blessed are those who mourn, for they will be comforted. Blessed are the gentle, for they will inherit the earth. Blessed are those who hunger and thirst for righteousness, for they will be satisfied. Blessed are the merciful, for they will receive mercy. Blessed are the pure in heart, for they will see God. Blessed are the peacemakers, for they will be called sons of God. Blessed are those who have been persecuted for the sake of righteousness, for theirs is the kingdom of heaven.'

This hits home for me. We are blessed with Jesus. We didn't deserve for Him to die for us, for we all fall short and sin, but He did and because of it we are blessed. Yes, life can be hard sometimes. It can be unfair, unjust, and we don't always feel blessed. The reality is, even in these moments we have a Heavenly Father who is good, who has compassion, and who knows our pain. The abounding love of Jesus and His sacrifice on the cross is the reason why we can sing we are blessed. This experience gave me the opportunity to reflect on my attitude, on my gratitude and on my own personal walk with the lord. They displayed a Christlike attitude for us to witness and I hope and pray we were able to share His light with them also.

As I have previously mentioned, in Southeast Asia, when it rains it pours. And when I say pours, I mean it forcefully buckets down. One beautiful sunny day we decided it would be a great idea to go on a hike with some locals. All of us were awestruck with the wonders of the lush green rainforest as we were trekking through the unpaved tracks. Suddenly, we heard the roar of a mighty waterfall. I tried to catch a glimpse of its beauty, but it proved to be difficult as I had to also look at where I was going. I am not skilled in this department. Once we got to the massive waterfall, I thought it would be a good idea to leave my phone at the base of the waterfall. Because, why not! And then, of course, we scaled the huge waterfall without any safety equipment on slippery rocks and a cliffside. I was lowkey scared and my knees were shaking, but I was also having too much fun to worry about the consequences. As I jumped over rocks and heaved and huffed my way up the cliffside, I was exhilarated, full of adrenaline and ready for more. Suddenly out of absolute nowhere, I saw a flash of lightning and my brave soul turned into a trembling mess. There was a storm approaching. I don't know if you remember, but I am not particularly fond of storms. As we were almost at the base of the waterfall it started to drizzle. I managed to snatch my bag and then the rain started to bucket down. We trekked for what felt like miles through the rainforest in the pouring rain. We were completely and utterly soaked, and my feet were making the squishing noise in the dampness of the forest. I have never walked in torrential rain before and to be honest it was kind of fun. I had a few valuables in my bag such as my phone, but I wasn't too worried about it because it was waterproof. However, my earphones were not. I was a tad concerned, but it didn't stop me from savouring the moment. Once we had finally arrived under some shelter, we were all soaking wet from head to toe. As we were drying off, I decided to look at my phone to check what time it was. I reached into my drenched bag and my stomach hit the floor when I grabbed my phone and it did not turn on. I tried again and it did not work. Now, ladies and gentlemen, if you are wondering, this is the exact same phone as the one mentioned in the previous chapter. I glanced at my iPhone, which was advertised as 'waterproof,' and to my horror I saw water droplets within the camera. Long story short, it did not turn on at all, it was dead.

Here I was once again in another country without a phone. I did not back up any of my photos. You would think I would have learned a lesson from my previous experience, but I did not. In this moment, I had to check my attitude. I could have let this ruin the rest of my trip as I still had six weeks to go, but I did not. I surrendered my iPhone and all of my photos to God because He is far greater than any photo I could ever take. I came to realise, oftentimes I would rely on my iPhone more than God. It is easy to do, because our phones are extremely useful, and we rely on them to practically live in this world. Not having a phone in this time taught me to rely on God rather than my phone for a season and it was refreshing and beautiful. Now, don't get me wrong, I think phones are great and I am not 'anti- phones,' but my point is if you rely on your phone more than God there may be an issue. He is our Provider and Sustainer, not our phones. As a young person myself, I understand the social pressures of needing a phone to keep up with social media and trends, and I think social media can be a platform to reach people and be a light. But, there is so much more to life than scrolling through Facebook or Instagram. I am not telling you to give up your phone. I am just encouraging you to seek God and check your own heart to see if you rely on your phone or Him. I know personally, I have to continually check my own heart and intentions as I can get caught up in social media. Trust me, I know this may be an unpopular opinion, but I have experienced great freedom when I am not addicted to my phone or the social phenomena, which comes from social media. When I was in Africa, the first week I was constantly taking photos of myself with the little African children. In the back of my mind I was thinking to myself how cute these photos would be on Instagram and Facebook. God in a loving manner brought this to my attention and basically said, 'O*pen your eyes Gabrielle. Are you here to make a difference on your social media account or to make a difference in the world'* I still took photos, but I had different intentions. I don't think it is inherently wrong to take photos and upload them to social media, but it all comes down to our heart posture and intention for doing so. My intention for originally taking photos was to upload them to social media so I could boast about where I was and what I was doing. Honestly. I am cringing writing this, but it was true. God changed my heart pretty quickly and now I take and upload photos to savour my precious memories and friends I make along the way.

I apologise for jumping back and forth here, but back to my original point of being in Southeast Asia without a phone. It was challenging, but freeing and beautiful at the same time. Whilst I would not recommend travelling without a phone, and I probably would not do it again by choice, it was an experience I will never forget. I had my phone in rice for a few days and tried to turn it on every now and then, but it did not work. If this would have happened a few years prior I believe I would have had a completely different experience. Because I focused on God rather than my circumstance, my attitude naturally was fixed on Him. I had the best time because I did not let my worldly issue affect my attitude and my joy was found in Jesus alone. Whilst I would have been over the moon if my phone turned on, I was happy if my phone never turned on again. Because I travelled to Southeast Asia with a bunch of Americans, I was a tad nervous about travelling home by myself without a phone. This time, I knew God was with me and had a plan. It was a day before we were set to go home and I had a strange thought of charging my dead phone one last time, at this point it was about six weeks since my phone initially died. So, I hooked it up and left to go out. When I came back, I decided to check my phone, and I almost fell over when it turned on! It worked perfectly, apart from some strange pink lines on the screen. That did not matter, everything else worked fine. My phone worked perfectly for my entire trip home. I managed to get home safely and then a few days later after I landed back in Australia, it broke again. I was over the moon, which is not something anyone would usually say when their phone breaks. But it felt like God had enabled my phone to work so that I was able to get home. I did lose a large chunk of my photos from both camps and various trips, which was sad but in the grand scheme of things it did not matter because I will forever cherish the memories in my heart. God is undeniably, undoubtably good. All the time.

| 13 |

Parsnips

Alright, you might be slightly confused as to why I have a chapter called parsnips. This is a hilarious thing to say, but parsnips have a special place in my heart, and I am excited to share why. Since I have left high school, I have had a whirlwind of an adventure, but I have also been indecisive about what I actually want to do with my life. The only perk about being indecisive is being able to experience a wide variety of different things and being able to relate with lots of people. I kid you not, this has been my experience with university. I started off in a Bachelor of Education, changed to Theatre for a day then back to Education. Then, I applied for Nursing, Paramedicine and now I am studying Human Services. In terms of jobs, I have worked as a baby-sitter, McDonalds crew member and crew trainer, Student ambassador at the university, Recruitment and Admissions officer at the university, camp counsellor, lifeguard, missionary, student teacher, parsnip packer on a farm, a barista and waitress, gym receptionist, and an author (if you count it). If I add my dreams just for fun, I have wanted to be a famous actor, hairdresser, owner of a café, CEO of International Justice Mission, police officer, air hostess (which by the way I am too short for), travel vlogger, nurse, public speaker, pastor, and again author. There is my resume, not that it's of any importance. The job I wish to highlight to you is packing parsnips in a shed on a farm. This is the most mundane job you could get. Every day I would wake up before dawn, chug my morning Maccas coffee, and cut parsnips all day. At the start I really needed to check my attitude for this job. I love adventure and spontaneous unexpected things, and this was the polar opposite. In my opinion, parsnips are not even a tasty vegetable, but each to their own. If you like parsnips, there is no judgement. If you don't know what a parsnip is, I was in the same boat don't worry. In the beginning, I was salty. I did not enjoy being there and my attitude was in the wrong place. But like always, God was faithful, and my heart posture began to change. There was a lady named Jill who is the manager of the parsnip shed. I love Jill and she is a big inspiration to me because her attitude reflects Christ. She is always loving and kind towards everyone and always displays a friendly, happy attitude. You could tell her joy came from within. Day by day I started to become happier being there. It was not my favourite job in the entire world, but I started to enjoy it more and more. One day, I thought it would be a good idea to memorise scripture. I quickly opened my Bible and wrote down the first thing I saw, which was a passage from Philippians 2: 1- 5. It says the following:

'Therefore if there is any encouragement in Christ, if any consolation of love, if any fellowship of the Spirit, if any affection and compassion, make my joy complete by being of the same mind, maintaining the same love, united in spirit, intent on one purpose. [3] Do nothing from selfishness or empty conceit, but with humility consider one another as more important than yourselves; do not *merely* look out for your own personal *interests*, but also for the *interests* of others. Have this attitude in yourselves which was also in Christ Jesus'

At a time when I was struggling with my attitude, God led me to memorise this Scripture, which I thought was random, but He perfectly planned. For eight or so hours a day I would say this over and over and over in my head as I was mindlessly chopping parsnips, until I did not need my cheat sheet. Now, it is stuck there and whenever I feel my attitude turning sour, I say this to myself as a reminder that my attitude should reflect Jesus as much as possible. I also used this opportunity to try and teach myself Spanish, I am not one to pry, but I can totally count to ten in Spanish now.

Looking back, I learned quite a lot working with parsnips and I found myself closer to God because I was seeking and relying on Him more. Arguably, I found just as much, if not more, clarity and direction from God working in parsnips than I did overseas because I had minimal distractions and more time to seek him by myself. Instead of sulking whilst cutting parsnips, like I once did, I started praying and listening to God. It changed everything. The first thing I realised is it is essential to have seasons of stillness and quietness to listen to God and redirect our focus to be more on Him. If we just go, go, go, go all the time, we can sometimes go in the opposite direction God has actually called us to go. Be still for a moment, seek God with your whole heart. He is always speaking, we just need to become better listeners.

The second thing I realised is not everything in life is about what you do. The wonderful thing about life is our character, who we are as people. When I was working at the university, I placed a huge emphasis on my job stature. I found my identity in the prestigious business ideologies. However, when I worked in parsnips my status was stripped away and I was left with myself. I was knocked down and rebuilt, letting God, our Gardener, nurture and guide me into the woman He wants me to be. You will find we are constantly growing into who God has created us to be. If you are aware of Gardening, it is not a one and done sort of profession, it is a gradual, time-consuming, beautiful thing. Whilst it does take some time, the results are stunning, we just have to be patient in the process. You may get knocked down in life, but God always has a plan to rebuild.

The third thing I noticed working with parsnips happened on my first day. When I arrived, everyone I came into contact with said hello to me. People I knew and people I have never met all made me feel a sense of belonging and community. On the contrary, I went to my church the following Sunday and I introduced myself to a lady. I asked her how long she has been coming to church and she said 10 weeks. I felt sick when she said that. I could not believe she had been coming to church 10 weeks and I had only just introduced myself. The farm put me to shame that day. On the flip side, I have done some church hopping in my time. I went to one church and afterwards I cried all the way home because I felt like an outsider and I did not belong. Look, I love church, I really do. I just think sometimes we can get so caught up in the logistics of church, or our friends at church, we start to miss the point of church. Do not lose focus of why we go to church, it boils down to our love for God and others. If you go to church and there is someone new, be bold! Say hello. If you have never ever been to church, do not be afraid, it is a great place and I am sure you will be welcomed and loved. I have been to some phenomenal churches around the world which truly do exemplify the love of God. In saying this, we are the church. The church is not a building, it is the people founded by the love of Jesus. To be more like Jesus we need to fix our eyes and our attitudes on Him.

A word that aligns brilliantly with attitude is gratitude. Not only do they rhyme, but they inherently work together. If you are thankful for things your attitude tends to improve. If you have a positive attitude you tend to be more thankful for the things you do have. I am seriously thankful. But, oftentimes I get so caught up in the busyness of life, I start to take my life for granted. I recently participated in a charity event where we raised money for homelessness and we then spent a night sleeping out under the stars in the freezing cold. Prior to the event, I was telling myself this would be a piece of cake as I have slept on the ground in Africa and next to literal cows in Southeast Asia. But, I was dead wrong for multiple reasons. Firstly, we used boxes to build a fort to sleep in. I am not very good at building a fort. Thankfully I had some help from a good friend. Unfortunately, we did not get to finish it before the activities. After the activities had finished my main friend who had come to the event with me had to leave because he was busy the next day. Whilst I knew some more people, they were all part of a tight knit community, and I was a little bit of an outsider. I headed back to my half completed box fort and I did not have the energy or the drive to finish it by myself, so I jumped in my sleeping bag and literally dragged some stray boxes over me. Naturally, I did not get a wink of sleep and I 'went to bed' earlier than I usually would because I didn't really know many people. As I was lying there in the freezing cold, under a pile of boxes, I felt invisible. I had people walk past who would accidentally kick the pile of boxes I was situated under. I overheard conversations I definitely should not have heard. It was uncomfortable to say the very least, but in this uncomfortableness my heart broke. I realised what it is like to be invisible on a small scale. I thought about all of the homeless people who I have walked past and just ignored or looked the other way because I was 'busy.' It was a bitter pill to swallow. The second we allow the busyness of our personal lives impact our ability to love God, others or ourselves, something really needs to change. The small act of looking the other way speaks volumes into that person's life as they would undoubtably feel alone and invisible. Our actions speak volumes. As children of God, I encourage you to not look the other way, to share a smile, to love those around you because we have the honour of being and sharing the light of Christ to everyone. Throughout the sleepout, I was cold and dreadfully uncomfortable. As I was tossing and turning in discomfort, I had these moments where I thought it would be easier to pack up and sleep in my car or drive the five minutes home. I was incredibly tempted to do this several times, but I realised just how privileged I really am. Some people do not have the luxury of going home to a nice warm bed when they feel cold. They do not have the choice. The fact I had a choice echoes the reason why we had to raise money and awareness in the first place. Now I am not saying we need to feel a sense of guilt here. But, rather I encourage you to think about your own life and the things you are thankful for. You will be surprised how this small act of gratitude can make a huge impact on your day. For example, I do not like grocery shopping in the slightest. For some reason I dread it every week. However, when I consciously change my attitude to reflect thankfulness it isn't actually that bad. I am thankful I can drive to the shops, thankful I can walk around and choose things, thankful that my card doesn't decline, thankful that I have a fridge to place all of the groceries in. I now look forward to grocery shopping and my attitude about it has significantly changed. What are you thankful for and how can you implement gratitude into your day?

| 14 |

Lord Surprise Me

As previously mentioned, I worked on the farm cutting parsnips. It is not the most exiting job in the world, but it was a massive blessing in my life. Which is why I am mentioning it again. Most days, I was bored out of my mind, so one day before the sun came up, I decided to pray a crazy prayer. It went something along the lines of, "Lord, please surprise me today." I then went about my daily business. Suddenly, I ran into an old friend at the farm, who I had not seen in years. We had a wholesome chat and it was amazing to catch up. As I walked away from the conversation, I felt a still small voice in my head say, *'Surprise Gabrielle.'* I stopped in my tracks. Stunned. I had slightly forgotten about the prayer I had just prayed only hours before. I could not believe it, so I decided to pray the same prayer the next day and the day after. Guess what? God did not fail. Every single day there was a new surprise, whether it was running into an old friend or getting free cake or even a bus load of kids coming to the farm. Each day was new and exciting, and I could not wait to see what God was going to do next. God managed to turn the most boring job into an adventure with Him. He opened my eyes to His goodness, mercy, and kindness by surprising me in the most creative ways. God works wherever we are at. He answers prayers and He is moving in our lives. He cares about the mundane parts of our lives just as much as our big ambitions and dreams. Just as a gardener tends to flowers throughout every season, God is with us through every season in our life. He in fact wishes to be a part of every season of our lives. We just need to open our eyes to see his tender love and presence.

One morning, as I prayed this prayer, I had a friend randomly message me. I had not spoken to this friend in years, so I was definitely taken aback. The very next day I prayed the same prayer and this friend messaged me and told me to apply for a job, what a surprise! I sent in my resume, thinking nothing of it, and I went about my day. The next day she messaged me again to say I got the job, without an interview, and I needed to start as soon as possible. Now, without a doubt, I was surprised. I immediately quit my job in the parsnip shed and started at the café. What an adventure! This café was one of the fanciest places I have ever been to. All of the sweets were covered with perfectly polished cloches underneath a gleaming chandelier. There were flowers and plants and lots of breakable things. To say I was nervous is an understatement. I could not believe I had scored a job in such a fancy place. Me, the girl who is clumsy beyond all doubt, unveiling sweets in glass cloches to fancy people shouldn't be a problem right? This job was a new adventure on its own and I had never experienced anything like it. I am not going to sugar coat it here (pun intended), this was a super tough season of my life. Whilst it was tough, looking back I can see how God was with me through it all, and the lessons He taught me along the way.

Even when I was working at the café, I prayed the same prayer asking God to surprise me for the day. But this time it was different. I didn't notice the surprise straight away. It was only when I got home or when there was a quieter period, I would think about the ways God surprised me for the day. Suddenly, because I was now super busy and pre-occupied, I hardly noticed the surprises anymore and sometimes I didn't even pray for them. I went from being super excited about God's surprises each day to hardly even noticing them. Even though, I didn't notice them straight away, God was still moving even when I couldn't see.

I believe as humans we go through different seasons in our relationship with God. Sometimes we are well aware of Him moving and can see all of the wonders He does. These seasons are amazing and should be cherished. But, we also go through other seasons where we don't see or notice the things God is doing in our lives. These seasons are trialing and difficult. However, this is where our faith comes into play. God is always moving, whether we notice or not. God is not subject to our understanding, He is far beyond our understanding, and He is not limited to what we think He can do. Just imagine the sun for a moment. On a bright and sunny day, it is pretty clear the sun is shining; but when it is a cloudy day, you never stop and question if the sun is there or not. You just notice it is a cloudy day and go about your business. My point being, just as the sun is always there, God is always there for us, shining in our lives. The difference is, sometimes when it feels like God is distant, we question if He is really there. Let me tell you, God is there during the sun, rain, storm, day, night and everything in between. He is there and He cares about all of our adventures, our mundane moments, our heartbreaks, victories and defeats; He is there.

Going back to the café job, I noticed one of the reasons why I was not seeing the 'surprises' was because I was too busy to cultivate my personal relationship with God. However, when I really had a look at my schedule, I found I was not prioritising God as much as I previously did. This meant I was living more in my flesh then in my spirit, which is an easy trap to fall into. Have a look at your own life for a moment. What does your schedule look like? Are you finding yourself 'too busy' for God? If so, you are depriving yourself of your main source of light and life. Not to be harsh here, but it is true. During this season where I was 'too busy' I felt flat and defeated all the time. I honestly believe it was because I was cutting off the nutrients I needed to thrive by surviving on my own strength. I was not relying on Him who gives me strength, love, and compassion, but on my own unreliable, breakable self. It's like a flower denying the water the Gardener freely gives thinking it can water itself. I know it sounds silly, but it is pretty similar to our relationship with God. The truth is, to really flourish in life we need God to be a part of all things. He cares about the little surprises in our normal day, just as much as extravagant adventures. Trust me, I have had some pretty wild adventures in my life just as much as I have experienced the mundane. Let me tell you, God is with you and I just as much when we are in our nine to five jobs, or our study, or our shift work, as when we are overseas, or on holidays, or on a mission trip. What matters is our heart posture, our intentionality and our relationship with God and others. Are we seeking Him with all of our hearts or are we just attending church on Sunday? What is your intention? Do you truly believe God is with you through it all? Do you know you are loved beyond all measure and there is nothing in heaven or earth that may separate the love of God from you? Think about these things, really. I can tell you a million times over in this book that you are loved by Him, that you are worthy, and He is with you, which are all very true statements. But, you truly need to believe these things for yourself to see a change and to flourish into the person you are created to be. Read your Bible my friend, pray, and seek him. I promise you, He is not far. He is waiting for the moment He can surprise you with his goodness, kindness, grace and most importantly love.

Looking back, I can see the many blessings that came from the café. While it was difficult, I made lots of new friends and rekindled old ones. I got to know my regulars and make them smile. I got to serve coffee to million-trillion-gazillionaires and people in between. I got to learn latté art, which is something I had been praying I would be able to do for years, and I got to learn more about who I am. Sometimes in difficult seasons, it is hard to see the goodness of God because our view is tainted by our circumstances. But, God's view of us is never tainted or swayed by our sin because of the cross. Let me say this again, God loves you no matter if you see it or believe it or not. At the time, I was asking God why my surprise was working at this job, I knew it wasn't for me and I wasn't thriving there like I thought I would. But now as I look back, I can see exactly why I worked there, and can see how God was moving in this season. As humans, we can be slow when it comes to seeing God. Sometimes, instead of seeing Him work in the moment, it may take us months or even years to see what He was doing all along. Even so, it is such a profound experience to see God moving in our lives and in the world.

When I was at the café, I still occasionally prayed my usual prayer, and sometimes I would see the surprise! For instance, one day I received flowers from customers, or I saw people I knew come in. Those moments were always such a treasure. One particular day, I prayed this prayer. I decided to catch up with my friend Adoniqua. She happened to work at a gym. So, I went to the gym, in my non-gym clothes and caught up with her. As we were conversing, a friend from high school, whom I have not seen in five years, walked in. Surprise! She told me to sign up for the gym, and then my friend Nicole who happens to own the gym, came in and told me to sign up. And well, I signed up for the gym. It doesn't take much for me to say yes to things. The next day I participated in a workout for the first time in pretty much two years. Let's just say I wasn't able to walk properly for next three days (on a side note, this is now hilarious as not even two years later I entered a legitimate powerlifting competition and received first place! Funny how life works like that). As I was hobbling out of the workout I stayed back to chat with Nicole. She was explaining how the gym was looking at hiring a new receptionist. I simply said it would be something I may be interested in one day. Then I went home. The very next day, I prayed the prayer. Then I went to the gym. I waltzed on in and Nicole and one of the other managers, met me at the door. "Let's have a chat," they exclaimed. Of course, I was all for it. So, we sat, and we chatted, and I thought it was a fun conversation. Until they started to talk about shirt sizes. *This is weird...* I thought to myself. Then, they kept on saying weird things of the sort. "Is this a job interview?" I piped up and said with as much confidence as I could muster. They looked at each other and chuckled, "Yes, you have got the job, Gabby." I burst out laughing. I could not believe I accidently had a job interview and got a job. This was the biggest surprise ever. The very next day, I had to break the news to the café. I was relieved, but somewhat sad at the same time. During my final two-week notice, I was excited about the new chapter of my life. I continued to ask God to surprise me each day, and He did. One day, I got another surprise. I received a strange text message. This message simply said: *'Hey Gabby, I have your contract ready to sign, please let me know when you would like to meet.'* This number was not saved in my phone. I was astonished and had absolutely no idea who sent it. As quick as a flash I texted Adoniqua to see if it was the gym. To my bewilderment it was not. I was thinking about if I had accidently applied for any other jobs, but nothing came to mind. So, I decided to text this person back, pretending I knew exactly what they were talking about. We were having a grand conversation about a time and place to meet and I went along with it. I thought it was exhilarating. After a few texts I finally figured out it was the uni. They gave me my old job back. Of course, I said yes.

Now, as I was quitting the café, I had received two jobs without even looking, without an interview. It just happened. Over my time, I have applied for many jobs, including my embarrassing CEO story mentioned earlier and even a few gym jobs. Every time I seek a job and apply for it, I never hear back. I have never received an email to say they have received my application. I am starting to think I am not sending them right, and that God knows exactly what He is doing. To be truthful, when Nicole first opened her gym, I messaged her on Facebook to see if I could apply to be the receptionist and she said there were no positions available. My dream only a few months prior was to work at the uni and the gym… Now look! I got to work at the university and the gym for a season. God took me on a detour and an adventure full of surprises and challenges. Just so I could get where I wanted to be in the first place. And you know what? I learned skills, fostered new friendships, and learned more about myself and the precious love of the Father this way. And while I didn't understand why I first lost my job at the uni because of COVID, or why I had to work every weekend at the café and miss church, or why I was struggling with my calling and identity in the parsnip shed, I can now see the growth from the journey. I now see God's purpose and heart behind it all. If I had never lost my job at the uni, I would have never started to pray the prayer that changed my life.

I still pray this prayer and God gets very creative in the way that He answers. One day in particular, I prayed this prayer right after I went to the gym and was all gross and sweaty. I then decided to go to a café before work. Now this café was super hip-hop fancy, if you know what I mean, and I felt like I did not match the vibe whatsoever. Anyway, I started to walk towards the café and then I quickly turned around to run back to my car, but then I turned back to the café and started to walk again. Like always, the onlookers probably thought I was nuts. Nevertheless, I gathered up enough confidence to walk into the café by myself, and I sat down and ordered. I pulled out my laptop to start writing in this book, whilst sipping on my latté and eating my eggs benny. Now, I am not the most elegant person, so I was getting hollandaise sauce everywhere. After I finished my breakfast, I abruptly closed my laptop and almost choked on my last sip of coffee. There was a napkin sitting behind my laptop on my table. What on earth! The note said, *'hey I think you are really pretty and I would like to take you out for coffee,'* and it had a number on the back. My heart mas pumping a million miles per hour as I was reading this while getting whiplash looking around the café. I tell you what, I can imagine my facial expression must've been hilarious. I was thinking, *'Was this for me or someone else?'* As I had absolutely no idea who had written the note. Wow! What a surprise. I was shaking with the suspense. This stuff does not happen in real life and my mind started to do the thing. You know the: *'What if this is the start of a love story?'* and, *'What if... insert cheesy thing here.'* After all this, I couldn't help but thank God because I was surprised beyond all measure. So, I did what any person would do in this situation. I texted the strange person and decided to catch up for coffee. Some people thought I was nuts, and to be honest so did I, but I was excited. Long story short we met and caught up and he was nice, and also a Christian, but we have not seen each other since that day. I still feel like I got to make a new friend though! I will forever cherish this memory because it is the time when God absolutely surprised me and answered my prayer in a way I did not expect, which is ironic because I literally prayed for a surprise. When you pray for something, God answers in mysterious and wonderful ways. He listens and He cares about the big things and the small things and following Him is the greatest adventure we could go on. I don't get a massive surprise like this every time I pray the prayer, but oh my goodness, my life would be insane if it worked like that. What I am trying to say is that in some seasons God answers our prayers obviously, other times He answers them in ways we cannot see or understand and sometimes no answer is the answer we need. No matter what, He knows what we need, He knows what is best for us and trusting Him in all seasons is the best thing we can do to grow and flourish with Him.

Now, working at the gym and the uni for a season had its challenges, of course. I loved both jobs dearly. The uni has been a massive blessing from God because it has allowed me to save an adequate amount of money to pay for plane tickets to America, and they always seem to take me back, time and time again. The gym, on the other hand, pushed me out of my comfort zone. I have always prayed for God to help me get up early and for a routine to help me exercise. Well... this job provided both of those opportunities. 6am is now a sleep in for me, which is something I never thought I would say. Nicole has also been a blessing in my life as she has taught me what it's like to show Christ's love in the workforce, and how to have boundaries as she grows her business. I once told a friend about how I prayed for a surprise every day. She told me that she would be horrified to be surprised each day and her ideal prayer would be, "Lord make everything go to plan today." So, if your prayer is for a plan or a surprise or anything else in between, I encourage you to just pray because He listens, He cares, and He answers prayers His way for His glory.

| 15 |

McDonalds

If you personally know me, you are probably not surprised I have a chapter in my book titled, McDonalds. I am notorious for my love for McDonalds and Starbucks, which is probably why I do not have a gallbladder, but we will get to that later. In Africa, one of the first things I did was google where the closest McDonalds was. I was absolutely heartbroken to find out that the closest one was in South Africa. Anyhow, when I was 14 years old, I acquired my first part-time job at McDonalds. For the most part, I loved working in a fast-paced fast-food chain, I mean what is there not to love! I was an overtly extroverted teenager who was constantly surrounded by a multitude of people and exciting new experiences. One of the most tender experiences being the warm, comforting feeling of being able to buy whatever I wanted whenever I wanted, without having to bypass it through Mum and Dad. Of course, this was subject to the somewhat irritating reality of barely being paid minimum wage. I seemed to love this newfound freedom I was experiencing. Funnily enough, I was quick to realise I now had some new responsibilities I never knew I had. Such as paying for my horrific phone bill every month which, undoubtably, led me to shed a tear as I had to part with my precious earnings. After about two weeks of work, I had come to the sober reality that I needed to be wiser with my choices. Through this, I admitted that I desperately needed my parents more than anything to merely survive let alone flourish and thrive in life. You see, when we first accept Jesus into our life, we tend to become exuberant about the newfound freedom we get to now experience. An apostle by the name of Paul states in Galatians 5: 1, that is it is in fact for freedom that Jesus Christ has set us free. Therefore, as citizens of heaven, we get to experience all the freedom in the world because Jesus paid the ultimate price for us on the cross. He was bound, tortured, and killed, just so you and I could walk freely on earth today. It is hard to fathom the complexity and depth of His abounding love for us. It is so pure, deep, and vivid. As a result of this love, we are no longer called slaves, but citizens or Sons and Daughters. We are quite literally, 'called to be free,' as Paul likes to put it in Galatians. If freedom and grace is God's gift to us, what on earth do we do with it? Well, referring to my story, we can sometimes let the idea of freedom get into our heads. If not careful, we may become self-reliant, or prideful, just as I did when I experienced getting paid for the first time. This poses the question, *Was I really free?* Yes, I had a job, but that job alone was not enough to sustain me. It was only when I surrendered to my parents and allowed them back into my life I was able to experience true freedom once again. The same principle can be applied to our relationship with God. Yes, we have irreversible freedom as a gift from Jesus through his death and resurrection on the cross. However, to experience true and genuine freedom, we must not rely on our own strength but on God. When we surrender to Him and allow Him to move in our life, He gives us everything we need to be able to flourish and live abundantly. Jesus didn't die so that we would live an independent, minimum wage life. NO, He died so that you and I could live an abundant, and somewhat crazy, adventurous life with Him. Even in the midst of hardships He has called us to be free. So let us use this freedom to live in unity with our Father, to flourish with Him and exemplify His love to others so that they may do the same.

I continued to work at McDonald's for five years and within those five years I experienced many highs and lows. Naturally, over time, I created a name for myself. For instance, when hosting a children's birthday party, somebody thought it would be a good idea to allow me to face paint. At this request, an innocent child sat in front of me and expressed in a cute, high-pitched tone how she wanted a delicate rose painted on her forehead. Immediately at her request I channeled my inner artist as I attempted to mimic the beautiful rose. My hands started to shake, and nerves ran from one end of my spine to another as I thought to myself, *'I can't paint on a blank canvas without it looking like a cyclonic disaster, let alone a child.'* After what felt like an eternity, I finally finished in what my eyes looked like a beautiful masterpiece. As I planed the big reveal, a small, but piercing shriek, sunk straight into my core. It looked like someone had straight out punched her in the noggin. Tears streamed down her face as she glanced at the picture she wanted, then at the huge painted welt on her forehead, then at me. The familiar heaviness of guilt washed over me like a tidal wave as her mother pierced her eyes directly into my soul. Needless to say, painting is not my forté. Among other things, I was also known as the clumsy one. One day at work I was instructed to fill the shake and sundae machine. For people who are short in stature, like me, McDonald's has a cage type contraption which allows you to place the bag of liquid gold inside so that you can easily pour it into the machine. They also have a stool so people who were under five feet can complete the task at hand. This one day, it was extremely busy and blistering hot, so everyone who came through the McDoors wanted ice cream. There was a sense of urgency to fill the machine with the mix so that we could continue service. In my mind I believed I was the perfect candidate as I scrambled to the back and retrieved the shake mix. As I reached the machine, I immediately noticed the cage was missing. As we were in the middle of a rush, I was in no hurry to go on a grand treasure hunt to find this helpful tool, so I decided to freehand it. I took the mix out of the box, and surprisingly, it was a lot more slippery than what I remembered. I slowly, but efficiently, stood up onto the step stool and opened the channel for where the mix was supposed to go. I started to untwist the cap and, at this stage, I could feel the bag slip through my fingers and my heart skip a beat or two. I tried to hoist the bag up into a position where I could efficiently pour the liquid into the machine. In that very moment my feet caved in on me. I lost complete balance and, as a result, I gloriously poured the entire shake mix down my shirt. The whole bag! It was absolutely terrible. The shake mix seeped into my socks, my hair, the floor, quite literally everywhere. The worst part was, I had to finish my shift. Forget the walking dead, I was the walking McFlurry for the remainder of my shift. I gained a lot of stares, but also a lot of laughter, which ultimately birthed my first saying, *'Shame is lame.'* When I am saying, *'Shame is lame'* what I am really saying is: if you ever do something embarrassing, but it makes people laugh and it brings joy into their day, it was completely worth it. Trust me, I have used this saying a lot over the years! Despite being known as the clumsy one, I was better known as the one who was happy all the time. Obviously, this was not the case all the time, but strangely enough, more often than not, I was genuinely happy being there. I thought it was exhilarating as I would sprint from one end of the store to the other to get food out in time. With coffee and adrenaline pumping through my veins I was notorious for almost bouncing out the service window trying to get the food out to my valued customers. To be expected, I did receive mixed reactions from my customers. I would often hear the remark,

"Why are you so happy working at Mcdonalds?" Or

"I want whatever drug she is on."

I would often have a sassy response in my head saying something along the lines of *'oh... it's just the Holy Spirit.'* Instead, I would shyly giggle and offer a warm smile as they drove through to the next window. Looking back, I could have used my drive thru window as an evangelistic weapon to share the gospel, but at the time, my strong teenage persona did not allow for such a thing to take place. Some of the more alarming responses I received were,

"I have never had anyone so nice to me in drive thru before" or even,

"I was having such a horrible day until I came through drive thru today."

This prompted my thinking and I realised that as members of the body of Christ we have more influence than what we realise. One of the other phrases I always used to tell myself is, *You can make or break someone's day by the way you even look at them.'* This proves to be true. By even offering a simple smile at someone it can change the trajectory of their entire day, as we have no idea on what they are going through. We are called to be image bearers, to share the love of Christ, to be his hands and his feet in this world. In my opinion, the McDonalds dining area or drive thru window can be just as spiritual as an overseas mission trip. My Grandma, for example, just recently handed out a Bible to a complete stranger in the McDonalds dining area. This just furthers my point. No matter where you are or what you are doing, you carry the fire of the Holy Spirit in your heart. What matters is your heart posture and your willingness to allow the Lord to move wherever you are at. No matter if you are a student, a teacher, a waiter, a CEO, a cleaner, a chef, or a missionary, we ultimately all have the same calling and that is to love the Lord with our entire heart and to love our neighbours as ourselves. Our secondary calling is the 'where' and the 'how' of getting to share this love with the people around us. The reason why I want to highlight my experience at McDonalds so much is because I want you to know that you can truly make a difference, with the help of the Holy Spirit, no matter the circumstance. I have spoken about Africa and America and all of these wild places, but you can also make a difference in your hometown. The playing grounds for where God can move is unimaginable. He can move anywhere, anytime. The only limitation is we tend to put God in a box and say, *'He only works at church or in other countries'* or *'He only speaks through those who are super spiritual.'* Who are we to tell God, the almighty creator of the heavens and earth, where he can and cannot work? I tell you the truth, whenever I am overseas, I wake up every morning and I say, "God how can I work with you today, God use me today to bring you glory." However, when I am at home, I tend to start my day with a quick thank you to God and then go about my business as per usual. The contrast between these two mindsets baffles me. Of course, I am going to see God move more when I invite Him into my day because I am consciously making an effort to see more of His presence. If we want to see God and flourish with Him, we have got to start inviting him into every aspect of our lives, our jobs, our family life, our study. I believe this is where the world changing starts, when ordinary people like you and I open our hearts, minds, and lives to the Lord and allow Him to work wonders in our everyday lives. We can make a difference where we are. We can lead an exciting life. I can tell you now that it is not easy, sometimes it is excruciatingly hard, but it is worth it, because He is worth it.

| 16 |

Storms

I am not fond of storms; just ask my housemate Amy, she can tell you about all of the times I have freaked out over a storm. What I am about to admit is embarrassing, but *shame is lame.* Whenever a storm would come in the night, at the first crack of thunder, I would sprint into my parents' room full of adrenaline because I was afraid of being alone in a storm. I did this until the ripe old age of 14. Sometimes, even now, if a storm is crazy scary, I may scurry into Amy's room. Unfortunately, storms are inevitable, just as the metaphorical storms in our lives are inevitable. I like to describe the storms in our lives as the uncontrollable events that come and pass, which are unpleasant and may do some damage. Storms can vary in size. Some are little and hardly do any damage. Some are hurricanes and can do some life altering destructive things. In my mind, a storm is a storm and it's all scary and unpleasant.

I am going to share one of the storms in my life and for this, we are going to stick with the theme of McDonalds. There is one shift at McDonalds that pierces my mind like no other. It was the 14th of August 2015, my senior year in high school. I had a night shift that ran from 5pm – 8pm, typical time for me during the week since I was heavily involved with school. There was a girl that I worked with and her name was Jayde. She was a couple of years younger than me, but we seemed to get along every time we worked together. She was great to work with. Of course, you can imagine, when having lots of teenagers from all different backgrounds together in one fast food joint, there tends to be an atmosphere of drama that lurks beneath the surface. There were a small minority of people that did not like Jayde for some reason. I have no idea why. To be perfectly honest, sometimes I can be oblivious to these things. I distinctly remember this one shift, just a few weeks before, a few of us crew members were in the break room and they were talking about Jayde in a negative way. I sat in silence for a few minutes taking in the conversation at hand, and then I finally plucked up the courage to squeak out these words,

"I don't know guys, I like Jayde!" Half laughing, they responded by saying

"Yeah Gabby, that's because you like everybody."

They continued with their conversation as if nothing was ever said. Fast forward to the 5pm – 8pm shift on the 14th of August 2015. I arrived at 4:45pm to make sure I was prepped and ready for the night. I slightly glanced at the roster and saw my dear friend Jayde was rostered on with me. As 5pm rolled around we all started to clock on to begin our shift. As I waltzed through the store to the service area to gather my surroundings, I noticed Jayde was not there for her shift and, apparently, so did the managers. It was a strange scenario as Jayde was notorious for always being a punctual worker. Nevertheless, at 6pm sharp she was marked as a no show and we made amends to continue with our job. Along with the constant stench of fried foods, there was a slight murmur that filled the atmosphere as the question on every one's lips was, *'I wonder why Jayde didn't show up for work today?'* At exactly 8pm it was time for me to end my short and sweet shift. As I was about to leave the vicinity, my senses came into shock as we all noticed that Jayde's Dad was there to pick his daughter up from work, but Jayde was nowhere to be seen. My mind started racing a million miles per hour as I attempted to rationalise plausible questions and scenarios of what I had just witnessed. I slowly entered the car and tried my absolute best to engage in small talk with my mother. Naturally, I was up for most of the night churning through my shift at work. The very next day, my heart dropped as they announced an amber alert for Jayde, which essentially means she was classified as missing. My anxiety levels skyrocketed like I have never experienced before. I had come to the realisation that the uncertainty of the unknown is what really haunts us the most. Jayde was classed as missing for two excruciatingly long weeks, and during this time, it was the talk of the town. Everyone's nerves were on edge as we were bombarded with signs, Facebook posts, and media coverages. It was an apocalyptic time period where no one knew anything about her whereabouts. Then came the 26th of August at around 6pm, when people gathered from far and wide into my church for a prayer vigil. Now, my small town of about 8,000 people is not known as a religious town, if you know what I mean. However, in this night of desperation, I witnessed people who have never stood foot into a church building fall on their knees in surrender to God. I remember getting goose bumps as the whole community gathered together to pray for Jayde. We tend to turn to things outside of ourselves when we lose control, especially when we experience unimaginable circumstances. For some it may be alcohol, others it may be relationships, but in that split second, in that chilling moment in history, my entire community turned to God.

The very next day I jumped out of bed with glee and excitement as I sprinted as fast as I could down my narrow hallway into the living area. I found myself surrounded by a culture of celebration as I received hugs and kisses and presents from my family. It was my 17th birthday, one of my favourite days of the year! I scoffed down my breakfast and I headed to the bus. I had the most wonderful birthday at school, people sang happy birthday to me, and I ate my entire body weight in cake. What a day, I felt like I was floating on cloud nine. For the most part, I had completely forgotten the matter at hand as I was in awe of everything. After school, we planned to go out for dinner. I was also very excited about this. I tried to make myself look cute as we scrambled out the door and piled into the car. We all participated in light conversation as the radio was buzzing in the background. I couldn't help but stare out the window, wondering about all of the cars that were flying past. I felt peaceful and happy to be with my family. Suddenly, my ears pricked up as my dad jolted the radio on full volume as it was the local news report. I heard three words that would pain my heart forever: Jayde. Was. Murdered. Shock horror filled the atmosphere of the car. I rapidly felt claustrophobic, like I was struggling to find air. It had felt as if someone punched a massive hole in my chest and ripped out everything inside of me. I have never known such a heartbreak, such a horror. My dad made an emergency stop at the shopping mall, and as soon as my deflated body hopped out of the car, I collapsed in the middle of the parking lot, heaving at the news I had just received. My dad rushed over to the scene and cradled me in his arms as I sobbed uncontrollably. When I finally had the strength to walk again, we decided to have KFC for dinner. Every bite of Kentucky Fried Chicken I had was pitiful. I could not comprehend how something so horrible could happen to someone as wonderful as Jayde. I could not help but think, on the day that my life is celebrated, the life of someone dear to me is commemorated. My birthday went from being my favourite day of the year to now my most dreadful day of the year. *'Where is God in all of this?'* I would think to myself, oblivious to the fact that he answered the communities prayer from the night before as He gave us some much-needed closure. As the days and weeks flew by, along with countless counselling sessions, and episodes of sadness, the harsh reality still stung. In moments of grief, I played the blame game. I blamed the guy who killed her, I blamed myself for not standing up to the people who were talking about her behind her back, I then went on to blame the people who were talking behind her back. Eventually, I blamed God. But God being the wonderful, marvellous, loving God He is, was always with me, even when I could not see. Even when the storm surrounding me was so great and mighty, He was with me.

After Jayde died, I hit rock bottom. This season continued until just after I graduated high school as well. I had no desire for travel or adventure. I was not passionate about the degree I was studying but I religiously stuck to it because I placed my value in what I was doing instead of who I was. The fear of being inadequate grappled my heart strings during this time as I envisioned my life. I always imagined that I would move to a farm, get married, have children, be comfortable financially, and have nice fancy cars. I also was only planning on going to church on Easter and Christmas. Sadly, I was putting God on the back burner of my life and focusing on the wrong things such as my boyfriend at the time and my status. I was acting similarly to how the Israelites acted when they were freed from Egypt in Exodus. It was clear beyond all doubt that God was with them, but they still worshiped false idols. As mentioned earlier, we are freed by the blood of Jesus to walk out in His promise that he has set before us. Imagine the timeline of our lives like the Exodus for a moment. We were once held captive by our transgressions and our sins, just like the Israelites were held captive in slavery. Then Jesus came and set us all free by giving His own life for us. We are now on a journey to the promised land or as we like to call it Heaven. Like the Israelites, we have two options. To either walk in this freedom and trust God in the impossible that He will provide manna from the sky for us or take things into our own hands and build false idols around our lives. Do you have anything in your life that you hold higher in your heart than God? For me, it was my boyfriend and comfortability. For others, it may be money or success. Whatever it is, these things tend to hinder our relationship with our Heavenly Father, whether we realise it or not. I thought I had everything that I ever wanted in the world, but deep down I knew something was missing. I was depressed. However, at the time, I did not want to admit it and denial was my best friend. I thought I was flourishing, but I was un-deniably cutting off the Gardener from nurturing me. Looking back, I had placed my worth and value in the wrong things. I had moulded myself to be what the world wanted me to be, instead of letting Jesus mould me into who He wanted me to be. There is always grace and love in the Kingdom of Heaven and no matter how far you run away from God, He is always with you and always loves you. I know this is something that is hard to comprehend when you feel like you are suffocating in the circumstances around you, but please know, He is there for you and loves you wholeheartedly, no matter how far you run away from Him.

One day I received a random message from a guy who works with an organisation that I have been involved with for years called Lutheran Youth of Queensland (LYQ). I have attended LYQ camps all throughout my childhood and they not only hold a special place in my heart, but also have helped me, as a child, to experience the love of Jesus in a fun and exciting way. This guy basically told me I should participate in a 12-day Young Adult Discipleship Retreat (YADR). At first, I was repulsed by the idea, because, you know, at the time I was not taking this whole 'Jesus' thing too seriously. I politely declined and went about my day. He managed to message me again, trying to convince me that this 12-day thing would be worth it. In dialogue, I conceptualised nearly every excuse under the sun not to attend: *'I have too much study to do'* or *'it's too expensive'* or I would even waffle on and say, *'I don't know if I can take that much time off work,'* even though in my core I knew it would be a piece of cake. He managed to counter-act every single excuse I could throw at him and, by some miracle, I made it to this retreat. God's will always has a way, and no worldly excuse could ever trump God's marvellous plans. Excuses may prevent us from following his direction, but our God is not limited by our rationality or worldly excuses. He is for the world not of the world. He can also work through obedient, God-fearing people. To say YADR changed my life is an understatement because it was God who changed my life and my trajectory. To be honest the times that impacted me the most were times when I just sat with Him. Yes, it was a lot of fun. We had rave parties, scavenger hunts, food fights, and I also managed to somehow smack myself into a glass door in the middle of the night.

These fun experiences were great, but they were nothing compared to the ultimate heart surgery that took place in my life. I had let my life become so consumed by the storms around me that I forgot what it was like to just sit in His presence. I forgot what it was like to praise him from the depths of my heart and to truly know that I am forgiven. I forgot how much scripture can speak and how it is filled with wonder. This retreat allowed me to take a step back and see the fingerprints of God in my life. It was where God revealed to me that we are his precious roses and he is our nurturing Gardener. It also allowed me to receive proper healing from Jayde's death. My heart was bursting with love for my Father and as a result I found that I could love others better too. I have always known God in my life, but this is the first time I really got to experience what it is like to have a relationship with Him. It is all because I pushed my own selfish desires and plans to the side and gave God the room to move in my heart. All this time, God had planted seeds in my heart that I have now been able to see flourish. I have allowed Him to nurture and grow me in his love. It is something I would not be able to do on my own. Just as plants need sunlight, water, and soil to grow, we need God to be able to grow into the sons and daughters we are destined to be. God has planted seeds in your heart too. Have you been allowing Him to nurture you? There is no special formula or equation to allow God to move in our lives, we just need to step aside and let him do His work. I am forever thankful for my friend who invited me to this retreat, but I am even more thankful to God for constantly showing compassion and grace to me in times when I didn't even acknowledge His existence. My life has not been perfect since this retreat, there have been many ups and downs, but God has always been my rock and my refuge. He is the most real and exiting thing in my life. It can be the same for you too! I am a rose, you are a rose, and we all belong in God's Garden (Kingdom) forever.

Since then, I have had many other storms in my life. After my first time at summer camp in the States, I was wondering why I was extremely sick all of the time. I was leading at a kid's camp back in Australia and one night I got severely sick. So, at a ridiculous hour of the night, my dear friend Nicole drove me to the hospital. They immediately hooked me up to the machine, and let's just say Nicole and I laughed all night. My mother on the other hand thought I was being atrociously loud and told me to be quiet. This was the start of a long stint of things going wrong. In the space of two and a half months, I had my appendix and gallbladder taken out (literally because of the American food), all four of my wisdom teeth removed, an abscess on my kidney, a minor car accident and was cheated on by my boyfriend at the time. I was in hospital for quite some time and I would class this as a storm in my life. I had to wear a Frozen operating gown because I was too small for the regular adult gowns. Everyone thought I was a cute child, but I was an adult. I was like one of those small puppies that growl when you think they are cute. Even in the midst of the storm, I was shown love by the nurses and doctors, my family, and friends and by God. It was where God stirred a passion in my heart for the nations as I would watch YouTube for hours, dreaming of the day I could fly again. It made me appreciate my health and also the love healthcare-workers demonstrate on a daily basis. It made me realise where my true joy comes from and that no matter where I am, even if it is lying on a hospital bed in immense pain, God is with me. I found my favourite doctor from this experience and he has been wonderful. He has even supported me on my trips. There have been many blessings that have come from my experience in hospital, even though at the time it was rough. God is with us in the midst of storms. Sometimes we recognise it, such as when I was in hospital, and sometimes we do not recognise it straight away, such as when Jayde died. Whether we see it or not, He is there.

It feels kind of ironic writing this chapter in this particular season of my life. I am writing this chapter with a bandage wrapped around my ankle, a few weeks after my mum's best friend suddenly passed. I don't want this book to bring you down, by all means. But, I want to be honest and say, sometimes life can be hard. For all of us. And while the Bible says over and over again 'do not worry' (Matthew 6:25-34 for example) and 'do not fear.' It also says, life will not be easy. A classic example being, Romans chapter 5: 3-5, where it says:

'And not only this, but we also celebrate in our tribulations, knowing that tribulation brings about perseverance; and perseverance, proven character; and proven character, hope; and hope does not disappoint, because the love of God has been poured out within our hearts through the Holy Spirit who was given to us.'

Seasons of trials and tribulations (aka storms) are inevitable through-out our life here on earth. Jesus himself suffered while he was here too. But there is comfort in knowing the spirit of God is with us always and that Jesus knows what it is like to suffer also. He has great compassion for us as He knows what it is like. I love, love, love being and serving overseas. It has been such a blessing in my life. Whilst I do not regret being overseas and I treasure the memories and the people, I have missed out on important events at home. I missed out on graduations, weddings, parties, and even funerals. In the two short years I have been overseas I have heard the news about my pastor passing away. My best friend Lydia rang me in tears during my layover to tell me about our friend Sjaan passing away. I remember weeping when I heard the news about my church friend, Malachi, who sadly took his own life. And then a week later when I heard the heart wrenching news about my dear friend Jake who lost his battle to cancer, which left me sobbing on the floor. Loosing loved ones is hard. If you have lost someone you care about, my heart goes out to you. Like I said before, a storm is a storm and they are all scary, so if you are going through any type of storm, please know you are not alone. I firmly believe what characterizes a Christian is how they act when storms rage through their lives. Now, don't get me wrong, I know sometimes in our grief we may blame God for the bad things that happen to us. I shamefully did this when Jayde died all of those years ago. But, when we turn to God when we don't understand and when our hearts feel like they are being ripped out of chests, He provides a type of comfort and love to us that nothing in this world can compare to. I just witnessed my beautiful mum shatter into a million pieces when she found out about her wonderful friend Janita. It was extremely hard to watch. But I have also seen God comfort her in a way I could never live up to on my own. I know my mum experienced great loss, but also great healing through the spirit of God. Annette is a person who I have always looked up to. She is the mother of Malachi. She experienced a severe trauma in her own life. But, I am constantly blown away by her strength and her unconditional love for God. I have never heard her blame God, but quite the contrary, she praises Him. She openly speaks about her experience and when she is struggling. I truly believe she unknowingly helps people in their own faith journey.

When I heard the news about my friend Jake, I felt sick to the stomach. I was mopey and sad, and I had no idea how I was going to get through such a time. He was such a kind-hearted person who loved God and had the most incredible singing voice. His hair looked identical to how Justin Bieber styled it in 2010, but I reckon he pulled it off better. We were work mates at the uni, and we would always talk about how much we love to travel. He was also one of the people who convinced me to do YWAM. Hearing the news about Jake hurt because he had just gotten married only a year before. His life was only just beginning, and it ended. Just. Like. That. I really sought God in this time because I had no strength of my own. I decided to do some Bible reading. I found a story in John 11, about a man named Lazarus who was a really good friend of Jesus (I have also mentioned this story a few chapters ago!). Lazarus fell ill and he died before Jesus came to visit him. After he had been dead for four days, Jesus went in the grave and raised him from the dead. What a story! There are so many amazing things to share about this story, however, the part that jumped off of the page for me were these simple words, 'Jesus wept.' He wept over the death of his friend Lazarus before He raised him from the dead. Note, it didn't say, Jesus shed a tear. It said He wept, which probably meant snot and all. Jesus knows what it is like to go through seasons of loss and pain and suffering. After this, I read the story about how Jesus was asleep on a boat with His disciples, and it started to storm (Luke 8:22-25). All of the disciples were deathly afraid, which I don't blame them to be quite honest, and they woke Jesus up. Jesus then basically told them they have little faith, as He told the wind and the waves to stop. I then went on to read about how Jesus felt the night before he was put to death found in Mark 14: 33 - 34:

'And He took with Him Peter, James, and John, and began to be very distressed and troubled. And He said to them, "My soul is deeply grieved, to the point of death; remain here and keep watch."'

Jesus, our Saviour, went through storms too. Some quite severe. Jesus went through all sorts of storms, literally and metaphorically. He knows what it is like too ugly weep over losing a loved one, or be betrayed, disliked, gossiped about. He knows what it is like to be in physical pain as He was brutally killed just so we could live. I mean He quite literally said His soul is overwhelmed with sorrow to the point of death. If that is not the definition of suffering, I don't know what is. From the three Bible readings mentioned above, it is the most comforting to know these two things. Firstly, Jesus knows how we feel; therefore, He has endless empathy, compassion, and love for us. Secondly, He is always with us during the storms we face. We never have to battle it alone. Even when our life is shaking and we feel our boat is sinking, He is there in the rocky boat with us, enduring the storms with us and bringing His ultimate peace.

| 17 |

Weeds

I don't know about you, but I hate weeds. They are atrocious plants, which ruin the beauty of a garden and if left unattended, can cause a catastrophic mess. Previously, I spoke about how storms are these uncontrollable events in our lives that come and pass. On the contrary, I like to imagine weeds are the negative things which may have been said to us or done to us, that make us act in a certain manner.

I love singing and public speaking. When I was in high school, I was the most typical drama kid. You know, in all the musicals, always on stage in the spotlight. I love and thrive off this sort of thing. However, for some strange reason, when I sing by myself or in a small group, especially in church, I get nervous and doubt my abilities. I shy away. When I get up to sing in front of people, I feel like I am constantly battling myself and my worth. I am still in the band at church and sing in front of people all the time. But, I always have the lump in the back of my throat feeling that I am not a good singer. There have been multiple times where I have randomly cried during practice or I lower the microphone so people cannot hear me as well as the others. Then, I get embarrassed because I shouldn't be embarrassed about such a thing. I can get up and speak in front of 1,000 people, easy! When I have to sing, it is another story. So, one day I asked God to reveal why I struggle with singing.

Soon after I started to randomly sob during singing practice. Flushed in the face from embarrassment, I quickly ran out of the room to calm down. It was in that moment God revealed to me why I felt uncomfortable with singing. I quickly grabbed my phone and started searching through old Facebook messages. I found it, the root of the weed. When I was in Grade 8, so a long, long, time ago, myself and a few of my friends were going to apply for Australia's Got Talent. We were going to sing. We were quite serious about it too. We had a song picked out, we practiced together, we even had some lessons! Right before we were going to apply, I received a message from a girl in my class. In essence, the message said I should not apply for Australia's Got Talent because I am the worst singer ever and everyone thinks it. We didn't end up applying for Australia's Got Talent and I forgot about the whole ordeal. Subconsciously, I did not forget about this message. It was the root that the enemy had been tending to for years and I had absolutely no idea it existed. To put my singing anxiety into perspective for you. When I was in Africa, we participated in a vast variety of ministries, including church ministry. One chipper morning, the crew and I went to an African church. This was the most lively church I have ever been to. That particular morning, I felt slightly sick, but because I hate missing out on things I decided to go to church anyway. This church service went for four hours and it was probably one of the most memorable and longest four hours of my life. We were assisting with the church service, which meant we were in charge of worship, the message, and we even had some testimonies lined up. About an hour into the service, I started to feel the sickness coming. I must have accidentally had some of the water. I had a minor panic attack, as I was looking around at the rickety concrete walls to find they did not have a bathroom on site. I was in the midst of convincing myself all was good, but then our band started playing worship. It was great, apart from the fact the piano was hilariously out of tune. Everybody in the church was laughing and as I laughed, I pooped my pants. Yes, that is right folks, I pooped my pants in Africa. I had no idea what to do, so I basically pretended like it didn't happen. The worst part is, right after it happened, I was called to the stage to share my testimony with the entire congregation. So, I waddled up on stage with as much confidence as I could portray, and I shared my testimony. It actually went really well. Afterwards, I told my team and they thought it was the most hilarious thing. And you know what, so did I. The reason why I share such an embarrassing story is because I actually felt more scared when I got up to sing in front of people than I did when I pooped my pants. That is how bad the weed from this simple text message had grappled me.

Another example of a weed in my life is studying at university. Now if you recall, I have been quite indecisive about what I want to study; hence, I have not graduated from a degree per say. I work at a university and I tell people all day every day about the wonders of studying yet I do not hold a degree of my own. A few years ago, my boyfriend at the time told me these piercing words that have stained my mind and undoubtedly caused a weed to grow. He said, "I will not date you unless you have a degree." Ouch. Now, as a young person, this statement, mixed with the societal pressures of holding a degree, caused all sorts of lies and nonsense to sprout in my mind. Suddenly, I felt inadequate because I was too focused on my own worldly image to acknowledge the fact I am created in God's image. I think degrees are fantastic and if you are currently studying, or have studied, I commend you. I truly believe studying what you are passionate about can help edify and glorify God's kingdom. I am actually a huge fan of studying. However, if you are in the same boat as I was and you are unsure or you are not passionate about what you are studying but you feel the need to get a degree to be accepted by those around you, I encourage you to check your heart and your motives. Are you fearing God and following His plans or are you fearing man and studying for the sake of studying to please others? The wonderful thing about the gospel of Jesus is that you do not have to do anything to be loved and accepted by Him. He accepts you as you are and from a place of acceptance we can go out and study, work, go on missions, or raise a family. Whatever it may be, when we do it knowing we are already approved by God's mercy and grace, we can freely flourish into who He has created us to be.

I love personality tests. I think they can bring great revelation and insight to help us love others well. There are varying personality tests you can take online. I personally love the enneagram. The enneagram is comprised of nine different personality types that intertwine. This test helps a person to discover specific behaviours, motivations, strengths, and weaknesses. I love it. And whilst I love it, it has funnily caused a weed in my heart. I took a few online tests once and it told me I was 100 percent extroverted and 100 percent type seven on the enneagram. Now, for those who are not familiar with this personality test, the type seven is described as: extroverted, optimistic, spontaneous, high spirited and scatterbrained. When I first received the results, I was over the moon. I thought it was the best thing I had heard that day. Obviously, I waved the results at everyone who walked past and told them about it. They all thought it was hilarious and so did I. After a few days, I felt as though at least someone would refer to me as the 100 percent extrovert. I was honestly thriving, probably mostly in pride now that I look back. Then, I had an off day. As in, I was tired, and I didn't want to be around people. I just wanted to be alone. Alarm bells started blaring in my mind because for once I did not want to be around people. As silly as this sounds, I started to feel a sense of shame and insecurity as I was questioning my whole entire personality. I was questioning who I was, yet I was completely blind to the unhealthy standard I was living up to. As I read more about Jesus, I was comforted to know that He spent a lot of time with people, but He would often go up on a mountainside and pray alone. He had the perfect balance. I thought to myself, if Jesus the son of God needed time to be alone and recharge, there is no way on earth myself, a simple human, could ever thrive by being around people 24/7. I know this is an odd example; however, I want to ask you what labels are you holding onto? What words have been spoken over you, which you now class as your truth? Do these things align with God's truth for you? The only thing that set me free from this weed was looking toward Jesus. When we look to Jesus, the weeds become exposed and removed and inherently we are set free.

Weeds tend to choke the good and fruitful things in the garden, and I truly believe the enemy tends to the weeds in our mind that deprive us of the good things in life. If not attended to, these weeds can grow out of control and do all sorts of damage. Luckily for us, God, our Gardener, is an expert at removing weeds from the root. He doesn't just snip the top off and hope for the best, if you know what I mean. He digs deep and removes the root or the source. For us, it is probably more comfortable if we just snip the top of the weed off and pretend it is not there. Truth be told, the weed does a lot of damage if it is not completely removed from the root. It will grow back, again and again, if it is not properly dealt with. It is the same principle in our lives. If we don't address the root of why we feel a certain way, we will continue to feel the pain or uncomfortableness over and over again. God helps us to identify the root and He gently rips it out and replaces it with His truth. He won't forcefully rip it out, but He will gently let us know that it is there. Our roots need some attention if we wish to continue to grow and flourish. With singing, for example, I still sing in front of people all the time and sometimes I still doubt myself, but I now know that it is a lie from the enemy. I can now identify what is from God and what is not. I can stand firm and sing for God's glory because I know who I am singing for now. I want you to think about your own life for a moment. Mark this page and take some time to pray about it, turn to Scripture. Examine your own heart. Are there weeds holding you back? Have there been things spoken over you that do not align with God's love for you? I know it is uncomfortable. But addressing the weeds in our own hearts will help us to experience the freedom Christ has destined for us through the cross.

| **18** |

Thorns

Have you ever gone through a red light before? Have you ever made a mistake whilst driving? I shamefully and certainly have. It is not a great feeling whatsoever. The first instance was when I was in America. Just driving on the other side of the road was scary enough. I would try and put the indicator on and the windscreen wipers would start going 100 miles an hour. I had to verbally tell myself at every turn, *'I am turning left, on the right side of the road.'* Naturally, after being there for so long, I finally got used to driving and they let me drive other people around. One day I was driving my beautiful Southeast Asia team to get some vaccinations for our trip. We were talking and having a grand old time. I was driving and this truck turned in front of me and we seamlessly followed. I thought to myself, *'oh that was weird,'* as I looked up and saw a beaming red light in my peripheral. My stomach hit the floor and I gasped. Everyone in the car was confused. I told them I had just ran through a red light and funnily enough no one noticed. I was still ashamed of what I had done.

The second time was in Australia. I was driving in Brisbane with my friend from Canada. We were talking and I made a turn in the middle of the city. As I made the turn, all of these people crossed in front of me and I had to quickly slow down to ensure I didn't hit anyone. Like the first instance, I glanced up and saw the red arrow gleaming at me.

My face almost turned as red as the light from embarrassment. I hope I don't get arrested for mentioning my somewhat reckless driving. My point is, I always pride myself on the fact that I am a good driver. But, no matter how much of a good driver I actually am, I still make mistakes on the road. The same principle can be applied in our lives. No matter how much of a 'good person' you are, we all fall short of the glory of God and in some way or another as we are subject to sin. This is why we so desperately need Jesus.

The concept of thorns refers to the outward things we do that may hurt others. Thorns are these ferocious pointy things that are attached to the stem of a flower that causes pain when someone touches it. Thorns are the worst and, unfortunately, you and I have them all over us. I am referring to the conscious or subconscious actions we do that hurt others. I have spoken about my season in the parsnip shed quite frequently, and I am going to use it as another example here. One day when I was working a long shift, I was praying to God as I usually did. Then, I suddenly felt the need to repent for all of the people I have hurt. So, I asked God to reveal all of the people I have hurt consciously and subconsciously. And let me tell you, God brought up everything and everyone. There were people coming to mind from my childhood, primary school, high school, and beyond, it literally felt like hours as I was repenting for the things I had done to each person. It was a hard yet humbling experience. Then I had the audacity to think, '*I wonder what other people's repentance lists would look like. Mine is nothing compared to such and such.*' God, our gracious Gardener, stopped me in my tracks and lowkey rebuked me for thinking such a thing. It is so easy to think of other people who are 'worse' than us, but in comparing ourselves to others we are living in self-righteousness and pride. We become so focused on the speck in someone else's eye when we blatantly ignore the plank in our own eye (Matthew 7:3). What a dangerous way to think. There is an illustration I once saw that changed my whole entire perspective on our sin. I hope I can give it justice. It was a drawing. The first half was a rough picture of buildings from a side view. The caption said, 'our view of sin.' The second half had a picture of buildings as if you were looking down from the sky. The caption said, 'God's view of sin.' The point? When we look at sin, we tend to categorise the severity of the sin. In most cases this is to make ourselves feel better about our little flaws. We think some sins are worse than others and, therefore, some people are worse than others. Truth be told, sin is sin and any type of sin draws us further away from God. When we start thinking that our sin is not as bad as another, we are sinning because we are thinking of ourselves more highly than we ought. Oh my goodness!! I don't know about you right now, but all of this sin talk is stressing me out. Fortunately, the love and sacrifice of Jesus covers a multitude of sins. Our Gardener has thorn proof gloves and there is nothing that can separate us from his love and tender care. He is not afraid of our thorns. In fact, He helps us to see the thorns we have so way may stop them from hurting others. This is why the love of God is so surreal. He loves us unconditionally, in spite of our thorns, and He encourages us to love others in spite of their thorns too. Whilst we cannot love people as perfectly as Him, He guides us and shows us how we may be ambassadors of His amazing love. We get to love people because He first loved us. Wow! What a statement. He paved a way to love us, thorns and all, to enable us to love others, thorns and all. Everyone deserves to know and experience the love of God and we get the privilege of sharing His love wherever we go. As Christians, we are not exempt from thorns, however we can recognise we have a loving Gardener who helps us remove them from our lives. God is not scared or intimidated by your thorns, there is nothing that can separate us from His love. Jesus died on the cross knowing all about our funky quirks and thorns because He loves us regardless. This is the gospel, where God loved the world so much, He sent His son to die for us knowing all well that we are some messed up, thorn filled people. So that we may not perish but have eternal life with Him (John 3:16). By accepting Jesus into our lives, not only do we get to experience the most ultimate love, but He helps us identify our thorns so that we may love our friends too.

| 19 |

Other Flowers

When I hear other people's stories I sometimes get jealous. I know it sounds putrid, but it's true. For example, one of my good friends once told me about an insanely amazing dream he had one night where Jesus came to him and he was awestruck in the presence of God. He said he prayed for three days and then it happened, just like that. What an amazing experience. I decided I would start praying for a dream too! It has been a solid five years now and I have not had one single dream about Jesus. Does that mean Jesus loves me any less? Of course not. Does this mean I will never have a dream about Jesus? I am not sure. But, I do know one thing, this experience has taught me about God's goodness and my humanness, if you may. You see, for a long time I placed a huge emphasis on if I had a dream or not and if I 'experienced' God because I saw everyone else experiencing God more than me. Truth be told, God is with me all along gently whispering His love into my life and He is doing the same for you too. God is not an 'experience.' He is our omnipresent Father, Saviour and Friend, our triune GOD. He is our source, sustenance, and light of our lives. Sometimes, He lets us experience His goodness in miraculous ways, which is amazing. But, if we rely too heavily on the experience or feelings of God when we go through a season of not 'feeling' God we can be unstable like being tossed in the waves. This is why it is essential to be rooted in love and anchored in a relationship with our Father through reading Scripture, praying, worshiping, and being a part of a community. These things help us to stay grounded, to not be tossed by the ideologies of the world, but to be firm in Him.

This is easier said than done. It is alarmingly easy to get caught up in comparison or to think, *'why doesn't God do (insert circumstance) for me?'* Then, our minds jump to the conclusion of how they are better than us, or more spiritual than us and we aren't good enough. Let me tell you something right now. We are not good enough on our own, but because of His blood we are. You are worthy enough because of His grace. His love covers a multitude of sins, including yours and mine. I used to be embarrassed because I felt like I didn't have a testimony. Like my story wasn't cool enough because I am a little nobody from a small Australian country town. Then I read through the pages that I have written, and I am like, *'oh yeah, that's right, God did do that super cool thing in my life, God does move.'* You may be reading the pages of my book and thinking why God doesn't move in your own life. I say to you, open your eyes and ears because He has been moving all along. He loves you so much.

I recently told my cousin, Caris, about how I am writing a book. Half laughing, she said shaking her head, "only you could write a book, Gabby." I straight up told Caris that we can all write a book because we all have a testimony to share. I think she was taken aback as she sheepishly giggled in agreement. I bet you, everyone could write a book about how God moves in their lives. Whether it be about supernatural healings, visions or dreams, or about the small gentle whisper in our everyday lives. Both are extraordinary because it is our God at work. However, not everyone is going to write a book because God had called us to different things. I know some awesome people and have heard some incredible stories, yet they are called to completely different things. In order to flourish in God's kingdom, we need to move out of a posture of comparison and into a posture of celebration, celebrating everyone in their own walk and journey with the Lord. I truly believe God speaks in a multitude of different ways, to different people. So, when people share their testimonies, people can be blown away, time and time again. Imagine if God spoke in one standard way to people. How boring! He speaks in different ways to different people to exemplify the magnitude of His preeminent stature to show us that He is God and we are not. It is quite amazing to think the divine God of the universe speaks to us individually. The sad part is we tend to deprive the supremacy of it when we question why God doesn't speak or move a certain way in our lives.

I have never heard the audible voice of God, but I know plenty of people who have. Two of those people being my parents. My parents have heard the voice of God and I have not. I used to be salty because I have always wanted to hear the voice of God and of all people, my parents! I now think it is such a wonderful privilege to hear their story and praise God. My mum for instance was home alone one day and then she suddenly heard the thunders of heaven roar as she heard her name, "Rachel, Rachel" being spoken to her in a stern fearless voice. My dad on the other hand has a completely different story. Don't tell him I am sharing this because he won't even share it with most people. If this happened to me, I would have put it on YouTube already. My dad is a typical farmer. If you have ever known a farmer or have been a farmer you will understand when I say, depending on the season, farmers work extremely hard, with very little sleep. One day, during peak spud season, my dad was working as he usually does. He was driving a tractor that had a huge potato harvester attached on the back. The back of the harvester has a place where four people would stand. As the potatoes would be picked out of the ground, they would move up a conveyer belt where the people at the back would sort through the potatoes and throw away dirt and stones. One particular morning, when it was still dark and misty, my dad and his crew were working tirelessly. Suddenly, my dad fell asleep behind the wheel of the moving tractor, unbeknownst to the people on the back. The tractor veered off of the bed and headed towards the creek bank. As the tractor was heading towards a disaster, God spoke these simple yet profound words, 'WAKE UP.' My dad jolted up out of his seat quick enough to realise the direction in which they were heading. He just had enough time to swing the tractor around to safety. God saved my dad and four workers that day. This could have been the worst day of my entire life, but God interfered and turned it into a victory. I am forever thankful God audibly spoke that day. God moves on the mission field, He moves in homes, He moves in stores, He moves on farms. There is no prerequisite for God to move. He is working in each of our lives for the common good, which is His will and purpose. We get to all be a part of His story because we all represent the body of Christ.

When you think of a garden your mind usually wonders to a vast array of flowers and plants, popping with vibrancy and colour. You would never associate a garden with a singular flower. This would be a pot plant. Whilst flowers alone are beautiful, together they are stunning. There is a small city in Australia, close to my little farming town called Toowoomba. I love this little city for various reasons. Firstly, it is situated on top of a mountain, so the views are always breathtaking. Secondly, every year Toowoomba holds a festival called the Carnival of Flowers. This is my favourite time of year. Everywhere you go you see an arrangement of beautiful flowers. People have gardens out the front of their houses for the world to see. Shops have all sorts of flowers around their windows and doors. The major parks are popping in vibrancy with spectacular gardens. There are food vendors, rides, and people everywhere. It is two whole weeks of organised chaos and the whole town blooms. People travel far and wide to come to this event. People from all over Australia, and I am assuming even the world, come to the small city of Toowoomba. I met people who traveled at least three hours to come to this event for a single day. Why? Because thousands of flowers in a magnificent garden is a spectacular sight. People would not travel three or more hours to see a singular flower. If they wanted to see a flower, they could just go to their local Bunnings or Home Depo (if you are American). Flowers are better together. Yes, they are beautiful on their own, but together they are something breathtaking, something spectacular. I bet you have never seen a bride with a singular flower in her hand. No, she carries a bouquet! A perfect assortment of flowers that accentuate the elegance and beauty of the day. My point is, you and I, we get to have a relationship with our Heavenly Father. We are worthy because of His blood, washed clean by His grace. When we stand alone before God, we are loved by Him. When we stand together, we exemplify the wonderful beauty of His name. We are better together. We are created to love God and also love others, just as He has loved us. We are beautiful alone, but we are stunning together, as a church. What a privilege it is to be a part of Jesus' church, a part of His Garden. But, how blessed are we that we get to stand alongside our brothers and sisters in awe and adoration of Him who gave it all. We get to walk with others in their faith journey and we get to show people they can also bloom in our Heavenly Father's Garden. Loving people and serving people is an honour, not an obligation. We should love others relentlessly because He has loved us first.

One of my favourite places, apart from America as a whole, South Dakota, Toowoomba and Africa, is an airport. Ok, so it is now safe to say I love a lot of places! I love airports because you are always going somewhere new, whether it be home after a beautiful trip or awaiting a brand-new adventure. When I first started travelling, I traveled alone. It was exhilarating and fun. One of the things I would do is look around at all of the people. There are always so many people! There are usually men in suits and people who are carrying one or two more bags than what they can handle (which in most cases is me). There are always families, sporting teams, school trips, and one time I even saw an orchestra. I love people watching in a non- creepy way. Watching the hustle and bustle of the airport is probably the most entertaining thing you can do in an 11-hour layover. When watching all of these people, I can't help but wonder if they know God, if they know that they are loved by Him. I sometimes get overwhelmed because I don't look at these people as just people, I look at them as children of God. They all deserve to be known and loved by our Father. No matter their story, background, or status, everyone deserves to know Jesus. We all belong in God's Garden and Kingdom, not just a select few. Everyone. The greatest way we can show people Jesus is by loving our neighbour. Sometimes, loving others well requires us to surrender our selfishness and pride. One of my fondest memories is at a homeless shelter in Washington State. We had been going to this shelter for a couple weeks and the aim was to make coffee for them and to build relationships with them. After going for a couple of weeks, you start to build a relationship with the regulars. One of my friends was a guy named Al, he was from sweet home Alabama. One day he looked quite sad. So, after some light chit chat, I decided to try and cheer him up. I swallowed my pride and I stood up on the table in the middle of the hall. Then, after a second of awkward silence and piercing eyes I started to belt out Jingle Bells from the top of my lungs. I looked like a complete goofball and the security guards were giving me quite the look. But, Al and everyone around him could not stop laughing. After I had finished, Al said that he had not laughed that hard in months. He basically thanked me for acting like a weirdo. What I would like to point out here is it would have been easier for me to just sit there and not get on the table and sing. You already know how I feel about singing. It would have been less embarrassing for me to just act normal. However, this moment of embarrassment for me exemplified love and joy to others. Love is a verb and it requires effort. Sometimes it is hard and embarrassing, but it is all worth it in the end as we collectively get to look more and more like Jesus. Now, I am not saying you have to embarrass yourself to love others. I am saying, sometimes to love well we need to put our own selfish desires aside and willingly step outside of our comfort zones. We are a part of a Garden, a part of the body, and we all get to be a part of Gods bigger story.

| 20 |

Fragrance

I have an issue. I have an extremely weak stomach. I can't handle anything, especially smells. I gag over the most ridiculous things, which is a shame because one of my many dreams is to become a nurse. I wouldn't be a very good nurse if I was in the corner gagging all the time. Smells are weird, they can either be enticing or revolting. You know how much I love South Dakota, so you will be shocked to hear that there is one thing I do not love. In Sioux Falls, there is a park, it is quite beautiful and peaceful. I would consider this to be one of my favourite places, BUT it is next to a meat processing factory where I hear their specialty is making hot dogs. If you go to this park on an off day when the wind is blowing in a certain direction, it is awful. The smell is horrific. It takes away all of the beauty because it is stained with a wretched smell. The downer is, the smell is so severe you can smell it from the airport as well. Yep, as soon as you arrive in South Dakota you are sometimes greeted by this nasty smell. All you want to do is hold your breath and run as fast as you can to safety. I feel like you need a complementary mask when you arrive to make the time at the airport or the park more enjoyable for the public. It is funny how a smell can change someone's entire perspective on a place. On the contrast, one of the reasons why I adore Walmart is because of a smell. Okay, before you put this book down and think I am nuts, please hear me out. I love Walmart for many reasons. There are so many aisles with everything you will ever need. It even has a grocery store which I have undoubtably mentioned before. My favourite aisle is the candle aisle. Now, I have never actually bought a candle from Walmart before. But, when I am feeling sad, I go to the candles, and I smell all of the different fragrances to make me feel better. No joke, I have stood in the candle aisle bawling my eyes out sniffing all the different varieties of candles. I then pick my favourite one. I can't even begin to imagine what the people walking past must have thought. There seems to be a trend where I cry my eyes out in public places when in America. Truth be told, there is something about a nice warm comforting smell that makes me feel a little better.

Certain smells have the power to either draw people in or drive them away. Do you wonder why people love flowers? Yes, they look pretty, but their smell is captivating. People love flowers because they smell good! Imagine if God created flowers to smell bad. Would we love flowers as much? Probably not. If flowers had a revolting stench, I would take one sniff and then flee the surrounding area until they are exterminated. Because flowers smell delightful, we can use them for special occasions, gifts, signs of love. You and I, we are God's creation, God's flowers, and we are a sign of His love. We get to carry the fragrance of Christ with us, wherever we go. We get the immeasurable honour of being the image of Christ and also the fragrance of Christ. What does this mean? Well we are not the literal fragrance of Christ, but just as a good smell draws people in, the fire of the Holy Spirit sets us apart and draws people into the kingdom. You carry a light that cannot be hidden, that cannot be tamed. Because your source of light is our everlasting, ever -present God, people will look at you and think, 'there is something different.' The way you conduct yourself, love God and love others will draw people closer and closer to our Saviour.

I was recently in Asia, in a country that is closed to the gospel of Jesus Christ. The main way to share the name of Jesus in these places is to show them how loved they are. A way to demonstrate love is to serve one another. Jesus, our King, even said He came to serve not to be served (Mark 10:45) There was a team before us that had been ministering in the same area we had been. One day, they decided they would clean out a local river. Unbeknownst to them, they had some people watching them. These people were a family from an extremist tribe that are radically against the gospel. These people simply saw the team of foreigners cleaning the river. But the Holy Spirit had a different idea. The dad of the family was baffled as to why a group of foreigners would be willing to spend their day cleaning a filthy river. It just so happened that the local pastor was nearby. The dad asked the pastor why these people would do such a thing. The pastor simply said, "It's because they love Jesus." The dad was deeply moved by this and he gave his life to Jesus. Then, his whole entire family followed in his footsteps. They got rid of their old ways, some of them were ex terrorists. They then followed the ways of Jesus wholeheartedly. Three weeks later my team and I had Christmas dinner with them. We got to sing carols about the birth of Jesus together, share a meal together, and we got to hear their redemption story. We got to hear and see how much they love Jesus and how much Jesus loves them. It was a beautiful moment to witness. I share this story because this is a perfect example of the fragrance of Christ. The team before us had no idea that their service project would bring people to know the Lord. But, their act of love for the people and their love for God was different to what the dad had ever seen. The love they carried drew this man in and ultimately drew him to know Jesus. The amazing thing is no matter where you are, you carry the fire and fragrance of Jesus. If you are called to stay in your home country, you carry the fire and fragrance. If you are called to go to the ends of the earth, you carry the fire and fragrance. There is something different about you, which baffles the world. You get the honour of sharing the love of God wherever you go. Sometimes, you do not even know you are sharing the love of God because it is something that flows naturally through you. You just need to stand firm in Him who gives you strength. There will be people and things of this world that will try to snuff you out, but the fire and fragrance that you carry cannot be hidden or tamed. Jesus died so that you and I may have a relationship with our Father and show people that they can be in relationship too. If you are in the word, in prayer and in worship, you will be representing God whether you realise or not. You may feel like you are just cleaning out a dirty old river, but God has other plans. When you are doing something that doesn't feel spiritual it doesn't mean God is not moving. He is always moving.

The astonishing thing about the team who cleaned the river is they have no idea what happened. They did not see the fruit of their labor. Oftentimes when I feel that God is not moving in my life, I open my own eyes and realise that it is me who is stagnant. It's me who is not reading my Bible or praying and then I blame God and ask Him where He has been. Who are we to question God and His movements? When I think of the word stagnant my mind drifts to mouldy bread for some reason. Why does bread go mouldy in the first place? Because it is just sitting around not being touched or eaten. And then, guess what? It smells bad! Seek first the Kingdom, seek first Him who sets us free. If you say you are a Christian, yet you do not spend any time with God and you are not cultivating your own relationship with him, people are going to smell it. Meaning, people are going to notice just like people notice a bad smell. Actions speak louder than words. What are your actions pointing towards? Another analogy we could use here is fruit. The Bible often mentions fruit. If you have good roots, you produce good fruit. On the contrast bad roots produce bad fruit. When people look at a tree, or even a flower, they only really see the fruit, the leaves, the petals. No one ever sees the roots, but they exist. Just as no one sees your personal relationship with God, they see the ramifications of it. People see your actions and the way you treat and love others. If you claim to be a Christian, but your actions say otherwise, what sort of picture is this painting for others? We are called to love God and love others with our heart, but if we are not doing these things, what is the point? We get the immeasurable honour of being Christ's hands and feet, to be his ambassadors. This is the most exciting, challenging, and exhilarating thing we could ever do. He loves you so much and He has assigned you the task of loving Him back and showing this love to others. Who are you going to be? Someone who is stagnant and stuck in the ways of the world, or are you willing to grow and be challenged to flourish into the child of God you are destined to be? The choice is yours my friend. But, just know, your actions or lack of actions speak louder than words.

| 21 |

The Process

This may be an odd concept, but I am going to share the story of how this book came to be. This is now becoming a book about the book, so it naturally is a 'Bookception.' I wish to share this as there is beauty and growth in the journey and the process. I hope it inspires you to grow deeper in your relationship with God too. When I was a child, I thought reading was utterly boring. I was one of those kids who would never settle down and take a break. Realistically, I think I am still the same; however, I have evolved, and I do like books. As a child, you tend to daydream about your future career and what your future life would be like as an adult. For me, I so desperately wanted to be a famous actor. The thought of reading a book barely ever crossed my racing mind and the thought of taking the time to write one would send shivers down my spine. Being an author was not something I had ever considered, but God had other plans.

As mentioned previously, when I went to the Young Adults Discipleship Retreat (YADR) I received the word of the rose, which as you know has shaped my relationship with God. But, another peculiar thing happened during the retreat. At one stage, I specifically remember one of the other attendees looking at me with bold eyes and telling me how he saw a vision of me with books. He encouraged me to keep writing. At the time, I thought it was a load of baloney, but what I had failed to realise is God was inevitably planting a seed in my life. This comment really struck my heart strings differently as I had never thought about writing anything. Ever. Slowly over time the idea of writing a book kept on creeping into the forefront of my mind. As I started to take my relationship with God more seriously, I started to have exciting adventures because I was aware of the things He was doing in my life. As you know, I absolutely thrive when sharing exciting stories with people. So, of course, I started to share the stories of how God was moving in my life. As I excitedly shared the stories of how I lost my phone or my passport or how I gloriously pooped my pants in Africa, I would usually get a similar reaction. People would laugh, shake their head and either say, "Only you would do something like that" or "You should write a book one day." I have had this happen so many times it is not funny, from Christians and non-Christians alike. After a while, I finally adopted the idea of the book as my own. The fire inside of me that wanted to be an actor slowly dwindled down into rubble as a new passion was ignited in my heart. God moulded my plans and ideas to shape His plans for my life. It is definitely not what I had in mind, but it has exceeded all of my expectations of what I had imagined my life to be. Oftentimes, I have seen people be scared because they think God is going to call them into things they do not want to do. And you know what? Sometimes God does call us into things we initially do not want to do. An example being to love our neighbour as our self, to the drastic point of our enemies. To give and be generous, to be humble, to only boast in Jesus not in ourselves, to pick up our cross daily. Honestly, the list can go on. My point being, there is a resistance between the flesh and the spirit, between heaven and earth, between the worldly things and Godly things. As much as we hate to admit it, some of these things do not come naturally to us. But, through a relationship with Jesus and looking to him through Scripture, as an example, we can be guided in the right direction. Then, after we spend some time in a relationship with Jesus our dreams naturally mould into what He wants us to do. Simply put, our calling per say, is to love God and love others. The exciting part is the how, where, who, what and when. Following God is the most exciting thing you will ever get to experience. It is also one of the hardest things because a lot of Jesus' teachings go against the grain of our human limitations and expectations. It also goes against what the world expects of us. There are no words to describe the wonderful love of the Father and the sacrifice Jesus made on the cross and what it means for us today. If there is one key message you take away from this book let it be that you are extremely loved by God and with Him you can truly flourish.

The idea of the book became more apparent in my life. Naturally, I started to brainstorm ideas and dream about all of the possibilities. However, it did not feel right. Every time I started to write I could not think of anything. I had a total mind blank, it was like pre-writer's block. I started to have the sinking feeling of sheer panic as I started to question everything. Was God really calling me to write a book? The answer back then, which I failed to grasp was, *'yes, but not now.'* When we think of the word flourish, we tend to imagine a beautiful flower, you don't naturally think of a seed or a little sprout. But, the interesting thing is, the flower you imagine has to go through the whole process from being a seed to becoming a beautiful flower. You can't plant a seed and expect it to be a flower straight away, it takes time and patience. In the same way, if God plants a seed in your heart, more often than not, you need time to grow and develop into the things He has planned for you. The concept of patience is uncomfortable because we live in a society that demands everything here and now. It is uncomfortable for me because I love and thrive on going places and doing things, all the time. But, it is well worth the wait when we go against our instinct and trust God for provision in His timing. God called me to write this book five years before I actually started to write a single word. It was a slow, but necessary process. Truth be told I am glad I didn't write the book straight away. I would have run out of content by page 17. When reflecting on this, I always think of Genesis chapter 15 and 16, where Abraham had to wait 15 long years for the promised child to come into the world. I can't even begin to imagine what that would have been like, those 15 years would have been excruciatingly long. At one stage

Abraham tried to take matters into his own hands and, even then, God was still faithful to his original promise. It is a true testimony of the faithfulness of God in His timing not our own. He keeps His promises, His way for His purpose not our own. You see, God may call you into something now or he may plant a seed in your heart that needs to develop first. In both instances God is good, and He rightfully gets all of the glory. Usually in these times, God grows something else in our hearts such as resilience, patience, trust or even friendships before we see the result we are inherently after. Or sometimes, we don't even get the result we are after. It's in these times He grows the things in our heart we didn't even know needed tending to.

I now wish to refresh your memory on the whole, *"you've got a book or two to write in you!"* email I received from Bob Goff, which continues to blow my mind and is another instance of where God was tending to the seed in my heart. Then, if you recall, I started to write the book and got to page 40 when God told me to restart because He had other plans. That was rough, but in hindsight I am thankful I did restart because this book is not about me. It is about God and His goodness and faithfulness even when I make mistakes (which is often). I have had a few setbacks writing this book and funnily enough almost all of them were self-inflicted. But, God has been so patient and kind throughout it all and I know if you follow the dreams which have been planted into your heart, He will do the same for you. Sometimes it will be difficult, but He will be with you through it all. After what felt like eternity, I started to actually write this book. Surprisingly, it was so much fun. After I had written a substantial amount, I decided to print it! This was a pivotal moment. I drove to Officeworks with the goal of printing my first ever draft. As I parked my car and scanned my surroundings something caught my eye with such force I almost forgot how to breathe. It was a gigantic painting on the wall adjacent to Officeworks. The painting hilariously and legitimately says, 'While we FLOURISH.' It was so big it was like a massive slap to the face. My hands were shaking as I tried to steadily take a photo of this sign because I did not believe it. It is undeniably the most amazing thing when God speaks. It can be in a gentle whisper or an enormous painting but when He speaks there is authority and power. I truly believe He speaks to everyone in different ways and I highly encourage you to be still and to seek Him with all your heart because He is actively moving whether we realise it or not.

So, after I printed the book and read through the pages, I came to the sober realisation that I had a lot of work to do. And I mean a lot. Hilariously, I didn't touch the book for a while. I started to fill my time with all sorts of knick-knack random things, but I somehow did not have time to write in the book. It was a peculiar experience because I had this tug on my heart, this persistent thing in the back of my mind, but I didn't do anything about it. As I was examining my actions, it was clear that I in fact did have the time, I just made a decision not to write because of my fear. Yes, I was afraid. I have a wide range of friends from different backgrounds and beliefs and I was scared because my stories are different. I love all of my friends wholeheartedly, but I truly let my fear of man override my fear of God. I started to seriously overthink the entire book idea and my book in general. My thoughts were, *'I don't have enough scripture and this group of people will judge,'* or *'What will they say when they read that story? I bet they will look at me differently.'* My brain would spiral into all sorts of wacky judgements until all I wanted to do was avoid the very thing that was planted in my heart and just watch Netflix. I then had the audacity to start a chapter where I tried to explain myself so that people wouldn't hate me. I call it the people pleasing chapter, and it is not featured in this book, but it is featured in our heart. If this is not addressed, it can bleed out into all aspects of our life. There is a difference between fearing people and loving people. Fear in this instance equals authority. We all get scared sometimes, but when we let the fear of man grapple us it deprives us of being courageous in faith. Do you have a dream you are avoiding because of fear? What or who has the authority in your life?

I found myself at a grinding halt, like an old truck revving at a crossroad making a life altering decision of turning left or right. I had the decision of either studying in semester two or taking a leave of absence to focus on the book. I was tossing up the idea, going back and forth, and back and forth like the waves of the ocean. It should have been an easy decision, reading all of the things I have mentioned it should have been a no brainer. But, for some reason I was grappling with the idea. It was hard to give up studying as I didn't want to look like a failure. It was comfortable to have something secure I was working towards, striving towards a degree to my name, and to graduate with my dear friends was an added bonus. Sometimes we are presented with these crossroad moments to see if we will go with our own desires and ambitions or if we will surrender and follow God, even if it makes no sense at all. I admit, it is easier to take the road we are comfortable with. If we decide to trust our own instincts in these scenarios, God isn't going to love us any less, He loves us unconditionally. But, I think when we take the easy road we are depriving ourselves of the growth, courage, grit, and faith we secure along the way. When we come to these moments and we don't understand and can't always see what's going to happen, that is when we flourish and grow with the Father. I have never regretted a time when I have been presented with a crossroad and have trusted God's way instead of my own. On the contrary, I regret the times I have not trusted God. It is funny to me how we trust our own judgements and take things into our own hands just to save a little bit of uncomfortableness along the way. The hilarious thing is, I do it all the time! We flourish the most when we trust God more than our own human instinct, which is a hard pill to swallow. I desperately wanted to enrol in subjects at university; however, I had this underlying feeling of discomfort and dissatisfaction that was looming in my brain. Again, I am not saying studying is bad, in fact you may have the complete opposite happen where you feel deep down you need to start studying. If this is the case, that's awesome! What I am saying is, God is calling us to an adventure where we need to trust Him and not our own desires. I was at war with myself trying to decide what to do. I had the wonderful thought of only taking one subject to ensure I was still working towards a degree. I was pretty set on the idea, but I knew if I enrolled in one subject, I wasn't fully surrendering my plans to God. I was gripping on to the idea of studying so much that I was not willing to let go for a season and trust that He has a greater plan. Partially letting go is dangerous because it alludes to the fact that deep down you are not willing to trust God wholeheartedly.

I have unfortunately been in this position many of times. Thus, almost enrolling in a singular subject at university. However, God always has a plan and a way to bring us back to Him. I was working at the university one day and it was like every other day in the call centre. I would talk to future students about their dreams, help them apply and laugh a little with my work best friend Nick. Just the usual. I work in the future students team. When a current student calls our number we transfer the call internally to the current students team and visa versa. This happens quite frequently, which is great because you get tiny pockets of time to chat with people from other teams before you transfer a student. I personally love when it happens. This one day I was speaking with a current student and naturally I started the transfer process. When I finally got through to the current students team a friendly lady answered. The first words she spoke to me in an excited manner were, "Gabby, I had a dream about you." I was taken aback as we barely know each other, but I desperately wanted to know more. What she said next nearly blew my socks off. She said, "In my dream I was reading a book and I had no idea who the author was and I flipped to the cover and it was you, weird right?" Because of my surroundings I tried extremely hard to contain my rollercoaster of emotions and I mustered up enough professionalism to say with a slight chuckle, "So you're telling me you had a dream about me being an author?" She chirpily said, "Yep" as I transferred the student. I honestly could not believe what had just happened. I didn't know if I wanted to laugh or cry or both. But, in that moment, I was finally convinced to not enrol in a subject for the semester. I hilariously think God was making it pretty clear on what I should do. It was like a loving, Heavenly slap to the face, to wake up to the things unseen. I had to surrender the comfortable thing to do, which was to study the degree. It was exceptionally difficult because I work at the university, which means I have to talk about studying every single day. But, after I had made the decision, I felt an overwhelming sense of peace. So, after this experience, you would think I would take this more seriously. Well, what a journey it has been.

Throughout the book writing process, I started off not wanting to tell anyone about it. I am not sure if it was a pride thing or an insecurity thing because I didn't want to fail. I did not want to tell anyone, which was severely out of character for me. As I started to finally tell people I was genuinely surprised. I had friends encourage me and check up on me to keep me accountable. I had one friend, Adam, who took it upon himself to become my 'manager' and literally every time I spoke to him the first words that would come out of his mouth were, "How's the book Gabby?" I would lowkey shudder because in most cases I hadn't even touched the book. He gave me a deadline to follow and I, classically, did not stick to it one bit, but he still encouraged me. I had my friends ask about it all the time and people willing to connect me with other people who have written books. I had friends at work ask me about it. I even had my non-Christian friends asking me and encouraging me about writing the book. I also had a non-Christian friend give me a book about writing a book. The support and encouragement I received was overwhelming and beautiful and it has taught me a lesson I will never forget. Being a Christian is not something you should do alone. The more I shared, the more I realised that God places people in your life to encourage you and to point you back to Him and His love. I have experienced the love of God through the love and support of my friends and family and it is something I will forever cherish. I want you to know that you are not alone too. Whether you are the person giving encouragement or the one receiving encouragement, you are not alone in this walk. It takes a level of courage to be vulnerable about the things you are going through or the things that you have been called to do. But, when you share these things with others, something beautiful happens, you help each other flourish. Now don't get me wrong, don't go sharing all your deepest darkest secrets to people on the streets, or walk around in pride bragging about the things you are doing. Rather, what I am saying is, find people who you can trust and who can speak wisdom into your life and, most importantly, people who can point you back to Jesus. We are destined for community, and we may fully flourish and cultivate our relationships when we love God and love others well.

After the whole dream incident, you would think I would write the book already, but I found a million other things to do instead. I binged watched Netflix, I started playing sport and going to the gym, and I got stuck in the routine of life. Every day I had a little small voice in the back of my head prompting me about the book, but I would flat out ignore it as I watched another TV series. It was rough because I knew what I had to do, I just had no motivation to do it and, therefore, put no effort into it (I just want to reassure you here, that I have in fact, put all of my effort into this book now). When God calls you to do something out of the ordinary it requires effort, faith, and courage to step out of normality and into the unknown. Faith equals action, and sometimes this action can be stretched so far out of our comfort zone all we can do is trust that God has a plan. It is scary, but worth it. To be honest, I was comfortable with the life I had created but I was not flourishing or growing. I got really sick and was unable to write for a while as well. I was scared because I was taking too long to write the book. I then had the audacity to think I had missed my chance and God took back the calling He gave me. I felt ashamed because I told all of these wonderful people about the book and my face would flush with embarrassment when I would say that I have not touched it. I was lowkey spiralling out of control to be honest. You might feel the same way about a calling in your life or about a situation you are in, and it's okay! God is loving and kind and wonderful to His children and I firmly believe He takes our humanness into account when guiding us to where we need to be. I am overwhelmed because even in the times when I have given up, ignored God, and tried to go my own way, God has never given up on me, and I 100 percent believe He will never give up on you. When I was spiralling, He rescued me. No matter how far you stray away or no matter what you do He will always love you and fight for you.

I have friend who is a huge inspiration to me in many ways. Her story is phenomenal. She studied to be an accountant and then God told her to take the GAMSAT test to become a doctor. Long story short, she took the test, got into medical school, and is now a doctor. She has also been a massive help in my writing journey. One day we were talking about the book and she looked at me and said in an assertive manner, "I think you need to enjoy the writing process a little more." I was stunned. It was such a simple statement, but it spoke volumes in my life. I had been so focused on the end result that I had not given myself a chance to actually enjoy the journey I am currently on. We can get caught up in the busyness of life or the goals we set, we deprive ourselves of enjoying the process. I am beyond excited to see this book published, but the process it has taken to get here has been phenomenal and I almost took it for granted. The lessons God has taught me and the love and kindness He has shown is something I will truly treasure. He is taking us on a growth journey so we can continue to flourish with Him. Flourishing is not a destination. It is a process and a journey and when we fix our eyes on the world and not on Jesus we miss these growth opportunities. I am continually blown away by my friends and family around me and the journey they are on. It is amazing when you have people to cheer you on and that you can cheer on too. It is hard to comprehend because we are each called to love God and love others, but the journey is completely different. Our varying journeys all point to our beautiful and wonderful creator which helps to paint a stunning picture of His complexity and love for us. I have friends who are passionate nurses, teachers, doctors, lawyers, YWAMers, camp enthusiasts, accountants, and mathematicians. I have multiple friends who own a gym. I have farm friends, real estate friends, youth work friends, friends who are wives and a friend who is a Midwife. I have student friends, retail working friends, marketing friends, and I have a friend who is studying a PhD in rocket science. I have friends who can sing like an angel and are wonderful artists. I have engineer friends, mechanic friends, parent friends, tall friends, short friends, cheeseboard enthusiasts, cake makers, wine tasters and everything else in between. You all know who you are and even if I have spoken to you once or twice you are my friend. This list gives me goose bumps because all of these people are on a journey and each of them share the love of God in different ways to different people.

God calls us to vastly different things and honestly some people on this list amaze me like no other. What truly amazes me is the fact that these differences truly glorify God and his goodness. It is exciting to say the very least! Now, if you are in the same boat as myself and do not really know what you are doing with your life, I encourage you to set your sights and sails on God and let him lead you to where he wants you to be. It may not be exactly where you initially want to be, for example parsnips. But, His purpose and way will continually out-shine our expectations. It is okay not to know because in the journey God inspires us to dream. He gives us different passions that contribute to the overall body so we may flourish as a community of Christ. We need to trust the growth process and trust in God's perfect timing and plan for our lives. I have massive outrageous dreams for my life like traveling to every single country in the world. I am not sure if it is me or God inspired, but what I do know is when we dream with God He exceeds all of our expectations. And who knows, maybe I might travel to every country in the world! What I have come to learn is sometimes God tells us things and gives us dreams where we have to wait and other times we don't. But, there is always a purpose. For example, the NeSoDak camp experience taught me the power of literally dropping everything to follow God on a grand adventure. This book on the other hand has taught me about God's love, faithfulness, and patience and my inability to be patient sometimes. We can plan all we want, but God's plan is far greater than ours and outside of our scope. But it's up to us whether or not we want to follow his plan or take our own comfortable path. God is not going to force His plans on us because He is not forceful in any way and we have our own free will. He gently lets us know His heart through Scripture and through His Spirit and we have the decision of if we wish to follow Him or not. I have done both and let me tell you, the times when I follow my own ways I feel numb, directionless, and all over the place. But, when I follow God, I feel alive, exhilarated, purposeful, and I feel that I can love people a whole lot more. You have a choice, and you always will have a choice, on this journey of life. It is my hope and prayer that you may see the love Jesus has for you on this journey and that you may know His great love for you always and forever.

| 22 |

Flourish

As you have probably gathered by now, flowers are breathtakingly stunning plants, which demonstrate all sorts of colours and designs. I apologise if you are a gardener yourself and I am completely butchering the terminology of varying plant types. Nevertheless, from my quick google search, I have found there are many stages to a flower's growth. They do not go from a seed to a full-blown flower overnight. It is a process, sometimes a seemingly long one. Interestingly, the term flourish actually means to 'grow well.' In the degree that I was studying, I explored the topic of human development. One of the key takeaways is, as humans we are always growing, whether it be physically, cognitively, psychologically, or spiritually. This seems like a simple concept, but I encourage you to really think about it. You are constantly growing and changing whether you realise it or not. You could be growing in a positive light or in a negative way. Just as a flower grows, mould and moss tend to grow too. The fact they are growing is the same, but the result of the growth is vastly different. You wouldn't particularly see a piece of bread with mould growing on it and think it is flourishing. In fact, you would be inclined to chuck it in the trash and erase it from your memory. When you think of flourishing you would think of a flower blooming in all of its beauty. Growth is inevitable, flourishing is a choice.

Flourish is a verb, not a destination. It's a way of life. Blooming is the flowering stage, which is the outward result of an inward growth journey. I have called this book 'Flourish' because our relationship with God is a way of life, and we get the honour of being able to grow in our relationship with Him because of Jesus. Growing with Jesus is the greatest adventure you could ever embark on. If you remember at the start of this book, I said, 'You will blossom and bring joy to the hearts around you and help other flowers to bloom.' You will blossom because of your growth in your relationship with our Heavenly Father and, as a result, you get to help other people flourish and bloom into who they are created to be too. Being a Christian is funny because it is both a personal and interpersonal journey. It is nurturing and cultivating your own relationship with God and, thus, helping to support and love other people to do the same. You are a member of the body of Christ. This means you have your individual place and calling, but you are collectively working with other people to form the body. What an honour!! It's about loving God with your entire being so His love flows out and you are able to love the people around you. How do you cultivate your own relationship with God? The Bible. The Bible is such an integral part of your growth and without reading God's word straight from the Bible, it is very difficult to flourish in a way that honours and glorifies God. The Bible is the soil a seed is planted into. It helps ground the flower and helps it to grow and flourish in the environment it is placed into. You can read all of the Christian books you like and listen to sermons and podcasts, which are amazing and I highly encourage it, but if they replace your own Bible reading there is an issue. This book is a tool to point you back to Jesus and the Bible. It is definitely not the Bible. It is inspired by it, but it is also written by me. A small 23-year-old girl from a tiny country town, filled with varying opinions and stories. I am not saying you shouldn't read my book, other books, or listen to podcasts, but it is vital you always go back to God and what the Scripture says in everything you do. The Bible is amazing (which is an understatement) and you should definitely read it if you are not already doing so. Another vital aspect of growth is your own personal prayer. I hope my stories have made this clear, but God listens to our prayers, He answers them in His own way, and He speaks to us all the time. When He speaks, whether it be a gentle whisper or as loud as a firework, it is radical, full of grace, and love.

It is my hope and prayer that you may flourish with God and continue to seek him first in all that you may do. I pray you may see His love for you, and you may go out and love others to help them flourish too. I hope you have enjoyed my crazy stories and know God wants to move in your life also. I hope that you embark on this adventure with Him and know that even when you fear or doubt, Jesus will never give up on you. I have said this over and over again, but He died for you so you may live freely in relationship with Him. You have the choice to follow Him and by doing so you will embark on the greatest adventure of your life. No matter where you live, what you do, where you come from, or where you aim to go, God is with you. He loves you and has a plan. I cannot express this enough. You have a story to share and a testimony which will give God the glory. You are a child of God, incredibly loved and valued. I wish to refresh your memory with the initial word I received years ago. I hope you know you are a precious rose and our Gardener loves and cares for you whether you realise it or not. He is waiting for you to say the life altering, Heaven moving, 'yes' to his love and plans he has for you.

'To my dear Sons and Daughters, you are like a rose with many petals. Each petal is something new and special. This rose will never wither, never fade as it is vibrant joyful and loving. There are many roses in the field, but each rose is uniquely different. Although some of your petals have been worn or torn, or you may even have some thorns; the Gardener [which is me] will water and replenish your soul and renew your spirit. You are a rose that can't be hidden, that can't be tamed, and you belong in my garden forever. I will give you all the nutrients that you need. I will fight off any pests or bugs that

may want to hurt you. At times you may feel that you might wither away, you might feel like you are ordinary. But you are not! You are unique and very loved. You will blossom and bring joy to the hearts around you and help other flowers to bloom. Love your Heavenly Father.'

www.ingramcontent.com/pod-product-compliance
Lightning Source LLC
Chambersburg PA
CBHW050942050726
47592CB00007B/2403